GET THI NECK WESHED

By Graham Shepherd

A Parson Cross/
Shirecliffe childhood

★ACM ЯETRO

ACM Retro
Published by ACM Retro Ltd,
The Grange,
Church Street,
Dronfield,
Sheffield S18 1QB.

Visit ACM Retro at:
www.acmretro.com

Published by ACM Retro 2010.

Graham Shepherd asserts the moral right to be identified as the author of this work.

A catalogue record for this book is available from the British Library.

GET THI
NECK WESHED

Longley Park

Shepherd clan at Farm Grounds Gala

CONTENTS

With grateful thanks to my wife Hilary for standing by me and supporting all my wild ideas for the past forty years.

Chapter One
"'s only me!"

Third of January 1945. A woman dressed in full wrap-around pinnie, tartan carpet slippers and obligatory head scarf over her curlers took a shovel from t' coil oil and went into her front room. She scooped out the blazing embers from the black leaded Yorkshire range and, ushering a few too many snotty nosed offspring out of the way, she went out into the freezing air and crossed Morgan Road in a pall of smoke. Opening the back door of number 28 with a call of " 's only me!" she ordered a six year old boy and his four year old sister to stand clear as she walked in and went straight upstairs to the front bedroom where she moved the old tapestry fire screen away and threw the smoking red hot coals into the cold grate. As the embers spread their warmth through the chilly room, its occupant, a chubby, jolly lady called Ada Shepherd gave birth to her third, rather inconvenient child, a scrawny little boy.

It was only a matter of time before news of my birth reached Adolf Hitler and his plan to take over the world, along with life itself, seemed to lose its attraction so he decided to jack it in, thus depriving my dear readers of several heart-rending pages about the blackout, the air raids and the absence of bananas. (You couldn't get them in the war you know!)

So that was it.

End of an era for Europe but just the beginning for a little Parson Cross lad.

Eighteen months and several tins of Ostermilk later a serious dose of pneumonia threatened to shorten this book to just one page. After a series of dubious home remedies had been pushed down my throat, held under my nose, applied to my neck on poultices, stuffed up my nostrils, rubbed into my chest and all to no avail, I was sent to hospital where I should have been sent in the first place. I would swear that at that tender age I can remember the sight of my mother in tears, leaving me there screaming pathetically, standing up holding the bars of the cot like a little thin, bedraggled prisoner.

In lieu of toys, Grandma used to put me behind her in the big easy chair with the previous night's newspaper whilst she sat knitting on the edge of the chair.

Perhaps in reality I only remember hearing about it so often from my traumatised mother that it has become fixed in my mind. Anyway after a couple of weeks I decided to give this life a second chance. And do you know it hasn't been too bad up to now, all things considered. In fact to be honest it gets better every day.

In no time at all my mam, out of necessity, was back at work in the pen knife factory, hence my first memories at less than three years old are of my days at Grandma's house where I spent the daytime hours. In lieu of toys, Grandma used to put me behind her in the big easy chair with the previous night's newspaper whilst she sat knitting on the edge of the chair. I have no recollection of reading the news but I would happily tear the paper into pieces, screwing them up and throwing them around. (Sometimes even now I feel like doing the same thing when I read the rubbish they print.) Anyway this went on until I was big enough to escape and toddle about getting into mischief around the house.

I recall on one occasion Grandma called me over and said that she was going upstairs to make the bed.

She took me away from whatever I was engrossed in and led me across the room to a big easy chair in the corner, behind which was a socket on an extension cable, plugged in to the wall.

She pointed to the outlet socket which was a bayonet type with two prongs inside and she explained quite emphatically that under no circumstances must I squeeze behind the chair, find the cable, pick up the socket and put my finger in.

She talked a lot of sense did my grandma. Now up to that point it would never have occurred to me to do any such thing. With that she went off upstairs.

I will omit the finer details and assume that my dear readers will accurately imagine a two and a half year old little wap being thrown across a room in a shower of blue sparks whilst contemplating for the first time the folly of ignoring the advice of his elders. Anyway it bloody well hurt.

Grandma had a tatty old dog called Mick. He was famous for walking on his own from Barrie Crescent back to Shire Green from whence Grandma had flitted.

(The phenomenon, still a mystery to science, is called Psi-trailing, but I don't want to show off.) Mick was a border collie, a daft, shaggy, gentle creature and generous too. When Molinari's ice cream man came and I asked Grandma if I could have one I was always told to ask Mick.

I would go over to him, look into those big dark eyes and ask if I could have an ice cream. He would gaze back at me and convey by telepathic powers still unexplained by science, that it would be fine. I would then climb up to the window sill, take down the old walnut money box with DOG LICENCE written on and shake out a few pennies.

I still treasure Mick's money box and there are still a few pre-decimal coins in there, but after sixty years the words on the box are getting a little faded. I have promised the wife I will clean it up when I get time but at the moment I am busy. I am writing a book, you know.

At risk of litigation I ought to remind my readers of a fact already widely known throughout Sheffield 5. Hurley's ice cream has got fog in it! Clayton's is OK. Molinari's and Monfredi's are no problem providing these feuding Italian families haven't had access to each other's supply, but Hurley's has got fog in it. Don't try it at home folks. Our Alan told me this and therefore it is true.

My memories of Grandad Joe are quite vague. He was actually a step-Grandad called Joss Akers and according to his marriage certificate he was an armour plate scaler by profession. That sounds like a real load of fun doesn't it! I remember him as a mild mannered old man, trousers up to his chest, collarless shirt, always sitting in the same armchair by the fire. I recall seeing him move only once.

I was running around and tripped over the pegged hearthrug, falling headlong into the white hot fire. I don't remember actually seeing him move then either, but he certainly did move. In a flash his comatose body flew into action and I was snatched away with just one nasty burn on my wrist.

This was soon cured with the application of more butter than would ever have been afforded for a slice of bread in those hard times.

Our Alan on three wheeler bike

When you think about it Grandmas was a pretty dangerous place.

As time went by my range of activity extended outdoors. Grandma's back garden, like many more, was uncultivated except for comfrey, mint and rhubarb but Mrs. Bruce next door had some ducks, or were they geese, which I would watch for hours on end despite the fact that they never did anything worth watching. I was also allowed outside on the road as there was never any traffic, but if a ball was released it would roll for ever down Barrie Crescent never to be seen again.

Across the road from Grandma lived two brothers who had learning difficulties, to use the modern parlance, though the expression of the day was less politically correct. Both were grown up and dressed like old men in very ragged suits, collarless shirts, 'weskits' and comically oversized caps. Jim was terrifying. He once threatened me with half a house brick until Grandma came out and shouted at him.

He was intermittently off the scene, presumably in some institution. Jack on the other hand was gentle like a little child. He drooled a bit and couldn't speak very well. He wondered around the area unsupervised throughout my younger life, joining in and talking as best he could to all the kids around. Everyone tolerated him to some extent and found him mildly entertaining but nobody actually accepted him into their circle. Years later he bragged to me in a quite mischievous yet innocent manner about some seriously improper activity with a young girl. He said it as though it was an achievement or a big joke and I didn't really believe him but soon after that he was never seen roaming the streets of Sheffield 5 again.

If someone had put inappropriate ideas into such a naïve head presumably they didn't think through to the possible consequences.

Get Thi Neck Weshed

But I mustn't jump to conclusions. Perhaps he maintained his uncomplicated childlike innocence till the end of his days.

When I was three or four Grandma and Grandad died within a few days of each other and my childhood memories drift away from Barrie Crescent back to the family home on Morgan Road. I have surprisingly few recollections of my parents in this period, presumably because they were both at work most of the time.

Only in my adult years did I realise with some resentment how they both had to neglect their children and work hard for long hours in dirty, unpleasant surroundings, not to get rich, not for expensive holidays not even to buy anything more than the necessities of life. They did it just to get by. It is a consolation to me that their lives improved steadily as years went by and, with some input from me, by the time they reached old age they were very contented people, deriving much pleasure from their family and grandchildren.

I started at nursery when I was three but during the holidays I was looked after all day by my brother and sister. Alan was ten and Norma was eight. In a modern world the three of us would be placed in care and our parents prosecuted but at the time nobody was criticised for working hard and ethics were measured by how hard. Children had to make sacrifices too, not that we recognised it as sacrifice, it was the accepted practice. In the mornings my mam would have very little input in the way of child care but would depart for work with a few basic instructions, ending with the immortal words.

"And get thi neck weshed."

I don't recall many problems except that occasionally, for reasons I can't remember, I refused to get dressed in the morning and Norma, assisted by her friend Marlene from next door, would spend half the day trying to persuade me, even resorting to a wrestling match on occasions. Not that dressing me was a complicated procedure. For most of my young life I was dressed in a type of dungaree trousers made from two identical pieces cut out from my mother's old coat and crudely stitched together around the edges and fastened at each shoulder with two buttons.

If only I had co-operated getting me dressed would have been a simple task of dropping me down into the pants and fastening the shoulder buttons.

Our Alan with Grandma's Mick

Fifty years later Norma asked me why I had a problem about getting dressed and I still can't explain why I was such a mardy bum. I think that once it became an issue I just would not give in - a trait that I am guilty of to this day according to our lass and my gaffer at work.

I can hardly remember the inside of the house on Morgan Road but some outdoor features which would normally go unnoticed by someone higher off the ground loom large in my memory. Just outside our gate was a slope between the pavement and the "causy edge." Part of the concrete had broken away revealing an area of very good quality clay. This was the one interesting square yard of an otherwise featureless Morgan Road and an equally featureless life. I would play for hours in the clay, which was ochre in colour and must have caused heavy staining to my clothes, but this was not my problem, my house had its own clay mine and I was a happy little boy.

The excavations gradually progressed and occasionally my mam would see the deteriorating pavement edge and say "Don't let the Duke of Norfolk catch you doing that!" I hadn't a clue who the Duke of Norfolk was and, in truth, I still haven't.

In fact I had only seen his counterpart, the Duke of Darnall, once in my young life. (He was a strange man in a bowler hat, pinstripes and frock coat, who kept Sheffield entertained for years by directing traffic in random directions around Spital Hill and the Wicker for no apparent reason.)

Morgan Road

Morgan Road was empty of traffic and safe except that on the other side lurked one serious danger. Over there lived an old man with a big moustache. Yes really! Every child on Parson Cross knew that old men with big moustaches were murderers.

It was a well established fact and I could never understand why the bobbies didn't come and catch them. but they never did.

Graham and rabbit

Perhaps they were frightened of getting bombed because on the corner of Morgan Avenue was a hole in the pavement which our Norma said was caused by a wartime bomb. It must have been quite a big one because the crater was at least six inches in diameter. Perhaps Hitler had a cunning plan to make the Sheffield munitions workers trip up and sprain their ankles on the way to work. Once a week we did actually see a vehicle on the road. The tea man would arrive in his Morris 8 van and we would go out to see him driving along and he would toot his hooter for us. He was a jolly character and we would skip behind him down the path where he would open the back door and call out the familiar greeting. "'s only me!"

On one or two occasions he let us climb onto the big mudguards and the hot bonnet of his van whilst he drove off down the road. Not a good idea I know, but we survived, and nowhere in the Highway Code is riding on the mudguard of a Morris 8 expressly forbidden. (You have no idea of the research I have put into writing this book.)

I can only remember having one toy of my own at that time, which was a furry rabbit, second hand, rather tatty and dirty but it was my rabbit and it mattered to me.

One day for reasons unknown and without asking me, my mother gave it away to Brighams, a nearby family with nine kids. A few days later I was most upset when I found it lying abandoned in the gutter on Morgan Road. Obviously the Brigham family were not concerned about the needs of defenceless woolly animals; neither did they care for the sensitivity of an insignificant little lad across the road. If I ever commit a serious offence and end up in court I will get a psychologist to tell the rabbit story in mitigation and the Judge will give me an absolute discharge and leave the court in floods of tears.

There was one other toy which was shared between the three of us. It was a small monkey whose eyes lit up when its tail was pushed in.

Get Thi Neck Weshed

We played for hours with this in the bogey hole, which was a secret space everyone knew about under the back steps, much loved by us kids. Eventually the battery and the novelty ran out, after all when you have pushed its tail in and released it a few times what else can you do with an illuminated monkey? Still, it was cutting edge technology at the time.

When I was three or four it was decided that we needed a bigger house and the time came to flit. Such was the efficiency and cradle-to-grave care of Sheffield Corporation that we only needed to ask and a three bedroomed "Three Winder" house was quickly found in an area of our choice just round the block, or "round t' lump" as it was called. I still pass the house regularly and it hasn't changed much, though nowadays it has clean curtains.

At that tender age the thought of life in a new house was of minor importance compared with the actual process of flitting. As every child knew, a flitting van was the biggest object in the universe and the excitement of riding in one was the equivalent of travelling to outer space. However, life was full of disappointments in Sheffield 5. How was I to know that the van was only for the furniture? All three of us kids had to convey ourselves round t'lump piled together on an old three wheeler bike. When I get to be Prime Minister it will be compulsory to extend the experience of young children by taking them in the flitting van when they move house. Surely children are more important than furniture.

I am told that when one of the flitting men was carrying a small wardrobe down a ramp I pushed a stick between his legs making him stagger comically for the length of our path to regain his balance which he achieved successfully without falling flat on his face with the wardrobe on top of him. I am sure I didn't do this out of animosity after they didn't let me ride in the van, in fact I don't remember doing it and would deny it ever happened but our Alan says it did so it must be true.

Herries Road. Graham's domicile from 4 - 24 years old. Now with clean curtains

Up at 'ut. First ever photo of Graham (centre)

Farm Grounds Gala 1957

Chapter Two
The luckiest family in Parson Cross

For a short while when I was a toddler we were the luckiest family in Parson Cross (which on the grand scale of things is not all that lucky.) We had our own country retreat! For fifteen quid my dad bought, from someone in the Magnet I think, a hut up Rivelin. It was a bit like a garden shed but had a brick fireplace. I don't know how we all fitted in but we even took other families with us sometimes. If you go to Rivelin Dams, cross the dam wall, then known as "t'Quarter Mile bridge" and go straight up the hillside towards Lodge Moor, you will perhaps notice lying in the undergrowth a row of old bricks and chimney pots from the fireplaces of the huts. Everything else was biodegradable and has now, well, biodegraded! I had to make a pilgrimage to find these ruins and convince myself it was all really true. What a nostalgic moment. If only it had all happened a few years later in my life I would have appreciated and remembered much more about the unique natural beauty and desolate magic of that magnificent place. The English countryside has only recently begun to resume its rightful place in my life and I am sure that the distant memories of those days "up at 'ut" have been smouldering in my soul all these years.

Behind the hut was a dry stone wall and behind that, a very dark pine forest in which were foxes, owls, rabbits, hares and red squirrels.

Yes, I did say red squirrels. After that the next red squirrel I saw was one hundred and fifty miles north and half a century later.

In front of the hut was a rough slope, a craggy outcrop, coarse grass, heather, bilberries and a mountain stream.

Inserted into the stream here and there were pieces of pipe where the water was allowed to tumble into sunken set pots. Filling the kettle was a simple matter of holding it under the continuous supply of natural spring water.

Some of the crags were massive. Despite the danger we pretended that one of them was a stage and held pantomimes on top, not that we had ever seen a pantomime. Apparently a runaway cow once fell off one of the rocks, killed itself and had to be dragged away, but my young eyes were shielded from this unsightly event to protect my tender feelings.

This didn't stop Alan and Norma describing the episode in full gory detail for many years after.

The hut itself was quite picturesque, having a small rustic veranda at the front. It was sparsely furnished with drawers and beds, all of which were transported all the way from Parson Cross on an old pram by my Mam and Dad.

The inside was lit by candles and always had an odour of methylated spirit, a smell which fills me with excitement to this very day. Evenings would be spent either up the hill at the Three Merry Lads or down the hill and "round t'ravine" past Wyming Brook to the back yard of the Norfolk Arms.

Here we would sit on bales of hay drinking pop and eating crisps.

These memories of all of us together, away from the normal bustle of life, interacting happily as a whole family, are very distant but precious memories indeed. Unfortunately my brother's asthma was blamed upon to the damp atmosphere or the furry wildlife and our country retreat eventually had to go.

After that, family holidays ceased never to return until I was old enough to take Mam and Dad away on holiday myself.

However, I was fortunate enough to take part regularly in that famous event, the Southey Club Trip to Cleethorpes.

That was a major occasion in my life and definitely required me to get my neck weshed.

Tickets were obtained from a club committee member who lived across the back, who I called Mister Vestibule due to his habit of standing having a fag in the porch doorway in his vest.

On receiving the trip tickets the next job was to swap them so as to get on the same coach as your mates. The networking involved in this would be the envy of a Masonic Lodge but by a complicated system of information exchange, success was usually achieved.

The trips were legendary and to this day you will hear many tales of the sixty coaches, the orange, the apple, the travel sickness, the half a crown,

the bottle of pop, the fish and chips, the "He's a Jolly Good Driver."
I wonder if anyone ever thinks about the logistics of all this. It never
ceases to amaze me that ordinary working class men, some of whom
were barely required to think in the course of their daily employment,
had the vision and the ability to buy land, commission a building, employ
staff, order stock, book "turns", sup seven pints a night and still have the
energy and inclination to organise a club trip for hundreds of kids. And all
for free.

To me it is a microcosm of all that was good about the working class. The
state provided well in those days but what it didn't provide, people got
organised and cheerfully provided for themselves.

If any Working Men's clubs are running similar trips today they will need
to consider a few points which didn't seem to matter way back then.

For instance:- Have all helpers had their police check, has a full risk
assessment been carried out, has it been read and understood by all
the helpers, Does every seat have a seat belt, has a home contact been
established for every child, has every parental consent been obtained in
writing, Is there a list of children's medical needs, are there any allergy
issues with any of the children and are all the foods and drinks therefore
safe, what are the insurance implications, is the club or the volunteer
legally liable. Is it any wonder that voluntary community activity is going
out of fashion?

Readers will note that this book makes the occasional reference to The
Magnet, a pub across the road from the Southey Club. The Magnet could
easily justify not just a book but a library of its own. However I have
attempted to relate in verse just a few examples of Magnet-related
anecdotes which came to my notice long before I was old enough to
drink there.

Thousands of Parson Cross people from several generations will have
their own anecdotes about the "Mag Oil."

It wasn't just a pub; it was the hub of the universe and a way of life for
people of my parents' generation.

I hope the following poem explains the influence that this den of iniquity
held over Sheffield 5 in general and my family in particular.

And every word is true.

The Magnet, Southey Green

There's a little place up Southey on
the Parson Cross estate
Not so much a public house, more
like a Billingsgate.
A sort of business centre with sweat
towels and flat hats
An unofficial Meadowhall – a
Selfridges – with rats!

My mother was quite certain and
she'd say without a doubt
That on a Monday morning you
could hang your washing out
And leave it in the sunshine all
sparkling and clean
And buy it back on Friday night at
Magnet Southey Green

My Dad said you could get your hair
cut in the public bar
Or choose your wife a present whilst
you sat and had a jar
But if you had a problem, all the
goods were "Sold as Seen"
And you kept your bloody mouth
shut in the Magnet Southey Green

Now me and my mate Weedy used
to play out after tea
Lone ranger (that were Weedy) and
Tonto (that were me)
Would be just about to draw our
guns and sort them baddies out

When from their kitchen winder
would come his mother's shout.
"Weedy, yer wanted. Come here I
want yer lad"
"Go and fetch me four milk stouts
and a pale ale for yer dad"

"Beer Off" was much nearer but his
mam was rather mean
And there's threppence back on't
bottle up at Magnet Southey Green
So our game was in suspension,
brought to an end too soon
Like them serials at Forum on a
Sat'day afternoon

When our kid took up pianner and
an instrument desired
The Magnet team in action soon
found one un-required
The transporting arrangement
became a minor hitch
Until to our misfortune, someone
suggested "Titch"
This rag man with a horse and cart,
who's business sense was keen
Was located, under't table, at the
Magnet Southey Green

The upshot was, the pianner, which
started in good nick
Was delivered by a rag man who
was five foot two – and thick!

Get Thi Neck Weshed

The Magnet in the 1980s

With his mate, equally lacking in
muscle, brains and charm
He was lacking more than that too,
cos he'd only got one arm!

Well the damage that resulted was a
sorrow to be seen
But they'd no complaints department
up at Magnet Southey Green

But my happiest recollection in the
Magnet's history
Was when Dad came home one
Friday night with a box of mystery
As he lifted up the cardboard lid our
eyes were opened wide
As a dozen chicks flapped round the
room – and my dad stood back with
pride

Us youngsters shrieked with
pleasure at this exciting time
(But my mam's words aren't recorded
for the purpose of this rhyme.)

So the old "Mag Oil" stood proudly,
the hub of the estate
But then it started getting less
salubrious of late

I read in't star one Sat'day night a
shotgun had been used
It didn't hit anybody but I bet they
weren't amused,
Except for 't landlord's missis, and
she was rather keen
It caused 'hundred pounds of
improvements to the Magnet
Southey Green.

Get Thi Neck Weshed

And still the tale's not over. The
goings-on prevailed.
The dodgy deeds continued when
the licence was curtailed.
That icon of the Parson Cross was
not allowed to rest
A few more crooked dealings still
had to be processed

One day the Wednesday football
team, already known for losing
Managed to lose their football
kit, (which the Blades found quite
amusing)
But firemen, damping down a blaze
at Magnet Southey Green,
Found the kit, down in the cellar
where barrels had once been.
And those courageous firemen,
those daring, brave gallants,
Saved the Owls the shame of
playing in their underpants.

Still not content to let the Magnet
die, one reprobate

Broke in to nick the brass door
plates. (It seemed appropriate)
He entered through a window,
hoped to drop down to the floor
But he was second on the scene,
someone had been before.

His predecessor hadn't got the
brass that he had planned on,
No, he'd taken out the floor the thief
had planned to land on
So down he fell to the abyss and hit
the cellar floor
(The football shirts had been
removed, as I explained before)

And there we end the saga of
dodgy trade and trouble
The centre of our universe is now
reduced to rubble
No dodgy deals, no purchases, no
more "sold as seen"
No preservation order - No more
Magnet Southey Green.

When I was three years old I started at the nursery at Shercliff School.
I will digress for a moment to explain that the correct pronunciation is
Shercliff, a fact known to old Shercliffians in particular and the world
in general, except for a very specific faction who by some freak of
circumstances all got jobs teaching at Shercliff School.
In their arrogance they persisted for generations in their attempts to
convert children and parents alike to their own upper class dialect
version, "Shire-cliffe." It has taken fifty years and despite each teacher
being outnumbered thirty five to one I fear they are gaining ground and I

Get Thi Neck Weshed

'Shercliff' Infant School in 2007

urge all Sheffielders to fight this at every opportunity. I'm sure that if the government can threaten that immigrants must learn English, it is not too much to ask that teachers learn the name of their own school.

The nursery was a terrible place. Even Benjamin the resident rabbit was totally uninspired, displaying no energy, intelligence or personality. Not surprising as he was even more of a prisoner than we were, epitomising the degree of freedom to be expected at Shercliff Nursery. On my first day, a defining moment in my life, I was taken there by my sister who was then only seven or eight years old. My mother was at work as usual.

I was given a smock with my own emblem on the pocket, which matched a picture on my very own clothes peg. Miss Morrissey asked me if I knew what the picture was.

"A house brick!" I declared.

Calling up all the sympathy and understanding this educated professional could muster for a terrified infant wrenched for the first time from the bosom his family and into her care, she snarled with disgust whilst I cringed in embarrassment, my bottom lip quivering. "It's a domino" said our Norma, relieving the situation a little, but it meant nothing to me as I had never seen a domino before. As a child born and bred in Sheffield 5, I had seen a few million house bricks, but no dominoes.

To be fair, in my two years at nursery I did have one or two pleasant moments. I'm not certain now if it was one, it could have been two.

On bright summer days we were allowed to take our little camp beds outside into the yard and snooze in the sunshine. In those days aeroplanes flew much lower and slower and made a droning noise for ages as they crawled across the sky until they faded over the horizon. I would lie in my crib half asleep

Me in nursery with domino motif on outfit

looking at the planes and imagining they were dropping bombs, which was, of course, what aeroplanes were all about as far as I knew.

On other occasions we would go and ask the dinner lady if we could borrow the dinner bell and we would march around the room in a line holding the back of each other's smock, tapping the bell and singing "Have you seen the Muffin Man" whilst having no idea what a muffin was. (And I'm still not sure. Is it a pikelet?)

Anyway this was the highlight of my life at Shercliff Nursery.

Some time later however, the sound of that dinner bell was to fill me with terror. Every meal seemed to include so-called cabbage, cauliflower or sprouts but I would like to know who was getting the sweeter, inner parts of the plants. Certainly not Shercliff School kids! We got the evil, obnoxious smelly dark coloured outer leaves which were not fit for a goat. One day I was confronted with such an inedible stinking mess that I simply could not open my mouth despite violent leverage with a spoon administered by Miss Morrisey who again showed her caring and understanding nature by taking me into the bathroom, dragging my pants down and tanning my arse till it was red.

Get Thi Neck Weshed

Miss Morrissey, if you are still alive and in your dotage somewhere, there are three things I want to say to you. Firstly, your approach was unsuccessful as sixty two years later I still come close to vomiting at the very thought of cabbage, cauliflower and sprouts.

Secondly I would like you to experiment with moving the corners of your mouth outwards and upwards sometimes. It is called a smile.

Thirdly, you must be overdue for your excursion from this world to the next. I would strongly advise that you do not look forward with any realistic expectation to a fanfare of trumpets when you reach the pearly gates. And if there is any hesitation about letting you in, just tell them to come to me for a reference. I am not a vindictive man. Well not usually, but I sometimes make exceptions.

By the time I reached infant school I had learned to keep a low profile. My recollections are few as the whole experience was easily forgettable but the highlight of life at Shercliff Infants was to play the drums in music lessons. There were clapper boards, triangles and other odds and ends, all with their own place in the hierarchy of instruments but the drums were the best of all. I have since estimated that I should have averaged a turn on the drums 3.3 times per year for two years. I am still waiting for my turn on the drums and my life is in ruins.

I took some small comfort from the fact that our Norma was in the junior school, within the same building. She was responsible for taking and fetching me and on occasions at the end of the school day I would sometimes end up in her classroom whilst the kids were still in.

All the class, especially the girls, would make a fuss about having an infant in their midst, stroking my hair and going "aah".

Me in 1st year juniors (neck weshed and posh jumper for photo only)

Get Thi Neck Weshed

The teacher, Mr. Mumby, unlike most of his colleagues, had a sense of humour and was liked by parents, kids and staff alike. He got all the kids going, shouting out that they wanted me in their class. I agreed entirely as I had never received such attention in my life and the prospect of being in Mr. Mumby's class removed any fear I might have had about moving up to the juniors. But it never happened.

When I reached fourth year juniors Mr. Mumby took our class for only one day. When he was out of the room for a while all the boys ended up brawling in a massive heap, for reasons long forgotten. When he came back and caught us it was clear that he thought it funny because he couldn't keep his face straight but he still made us form a long line, all touching our toes whilst he went along the line whacking us hard on the backside with an oversized gym slipper. I am strongly against physical punishment of children and hate to hear those adults who must think they are perfect when they declare "It didn't do me any harm" but I can easily forgive Mr. Mumby for this incident. Perhaps I was at least thankful to be noticed by the man and happy for any contact with him, even if the contact was via the wrong end of a gym slipper.

Me in 3rd year juniors
(best shirt for photo.
Only one lapel tattered)

I was not very well behaved in the juniors and would lark about in class instead of paying attention. I wanted to see humour in everything and this often led to disruption. One teacher, Miss Sloper had no control at all despite a fearsome, witch like appearance. My mate Gus and I would follow her down to the bus stop after school, saying rude things behind her back, which she would pretend not to hear because she was off duty. This lulled me into a false sense of security and one day we followed Mr. Spooner in the same way.

Using all the sparkling wit and repartee I could muster, I came out with a real gem of hilarity, loud enough to be heard.

"D.S.-DAFT SPOONER!"

Why don't teachers behave consistently? Instead of ignoring me in the manner of Miss Sloper, he whipped round, fuming, but being reluctant to administer violence in a public place, he said,

"YOU BOY! COME AND SEE ME IN MY ROOM TOMORROW."

I never slept that night and even the thought of going alone into the fourth year corridor filled me with dread. When I eventually mustered up the courage to see him, it gradually became clear that he had forgotten what it was all about. As I tried to mumble an explanation he said,

"Right, by tomorrow morning I want a written account of what you did, when you did it, where you did it, why you did it, how you did it...."

and a lot of similar things which I just couldn't take in as I stood there trembling. That night I wrote out a couple of paragraphs and then, lost for words I filled two foolscap pages with the lines,

"I MUST NOT CALL MISTER SPOONER DAFT."

When I handed it to him he perused the sheets with the usual stern look on his face except that just possibly, almost imperceptibly, there might have been just the slightest, tiniest, faintest hint of stifled laughter in his eyes. And I didn't get the cane. I no longer think Mr. D. Spooner is daft.

I wasn't always that lucky. One day in assembly we all had a lecture about not going on the school roof to recover balls. The message could not have been clearer but on return from dinner I saw Newty was on the roof so I decided to climb up and join him, thinking that the morning lecture must have been rescinded or delivered in error or not to be taken seriously or whatever.

Four strokes of the cane later I realised otherwise. There is a popular expression that people can "stumble blindly" into problems. Sometimes I was capable of leaping headlong into problems with my eyes wide open. We were always told how lucky we were to have such a modern school building. The futility of telling a ten year old that a twenty year old school was modern was beyond the understanding of our educators.

However the building did have one redeeming feature. Just like the most famous educational establishments in the world, ours sported a magnificent quadrangle. This architectural masterpiece, this wonderful, peaceful haven of calm was an ideal sheltered place for a troubled young mind to spend a few tranquil moments in serene contemplation. The pond in the centre was an oasis, presenting a marvellous opportunity to study a rich biodiversity of aquatic life not available in any other part of our immediate environment.

What a shame that the access doors were permanently locked and throughout my school life no child was ever allowed to set foot on the hallowed ground of the quadrangle. It was just too good for us.

A couple of years ago, on a nostalgic ride-around on my old BSA, I noticed that the school roof was covered with razor wire. It may have been put there to stop kids escaping because nobody would ever want to break in. It could have also been there to stop kids going on the roof for a ball because the teachers are no longer allowed to use the cane, which was much cheaper than razor wire. Whatever the reason I am sure that the visual impression given to frightened little waifs on their first day must take all the rest of their school years to overcome.

Unable to believe what I had seen I ventured that way again recently. The razor wire has not been a successful deterrent. Someone has now nicked the entire junior school! It has gone. But not to worry. Just up the hill is a brand new replacement called Watercliffe Meadow and from what I have heard it seems to be a stimulating and exciting place to be. Eee, these kids don't know they're born today.

Getting the cane was no more than an occupational hazard and the punishment did not have to fit the crime. There was no consistency. One day in the Seniors we had a stand-in teacher we called Dickie Valentine. He seemed to be giving all his attention to his girlie fan club and none to me, so I resorted to blowing down the edge of my exercise book to make that wailing sound, as you all must have done in class. Or was it just me? Dickie Valentine still ignored me for a while and then politely asked me to go down the corridor to his room and fetch his cane out of his cupboard. As I had not received an informal verbal warning or been given the opportunity to deny guilt or elect a supporting representative of my choice, I thought it was perhaps a bluff and my real punishment was the trudge down the corridor to fetch the cane. Three strokes later I realised otherwise. Sorry Dickie Valentine, I have learned my lesson. I didn't mean to interrupt your moment of girlie adulation.

This was nothing compared to the whacking Fats Evans got from the head teacher just for having a quiet fag. Traditionally the maximum even for murder was six strokes but the sadistic sod administered eight which nearly left Fats Evans' fingers scattered on the floor.

Mr. Dobbins then explained to the assembled masses that if anyone else wanted to use the "just trying it out" excuse they could go to his office and try a cigarette, a cigar or his pipe. In other words the two faced bastard was the self confessed biggest nicotine addict in the whole school. (Except for Fats Evans of course!) I'm sure that in the after-life Mr. Dobbins will not be short of a light for his fag, pipe or cigar. And to the pro-caning brigade I have to say that to my knowledge Fats Evans continued to smoke well into his adulthood, which I presume was not a very long one. (Though after the caning he probably had difficulty gripping his fag and striking matches.)

Mr. Dobbins' hypocrisy was again revealed years later when he featured in a picture in The Star wearing a big black beard. On an earlier occasion a young teacher arrived after the six week holidays with a rather becoming goatee and Mr. Dobbins sent him home to shave it off. (But diplomacy prevailed with respect to the women teachers - their beards were never criticised.)

I tend to dislike officiousness and pointless bureaucracy in all its forms (did you guess?) and one particular incident at school filled me with great delight. The deputy head took assembly one day and went to great lengths to reiterate the new rule as explained by the head teacher at the previous day's assembly, to the effect that all pupils must henceforth walk on the left hand side of the corridor at all times so as to avoid injurious collisions, noisy altercations and general chaos.

"Have you got that," he emphasised,

"WALK ON THE LEFT HAND SIDE OF THE CORRIDOR FROM NOW ON"

The one small but rather significant snag was that on the previous day the head teacher had given the same message with twice the emphasis, except that he had said walk on the RIGHT!

There was only one possible outcome, or should that be four? We obeyed and disobeyed both rules as appropriate and inappropriate. If we went up the left hand side and another class approached on the other side there would be a serious likelihood of not having a mass brawl, so we would cross over, obeying rule (1a.) and chaos would ensue. If however they approached on our side we would continue, steadfastly obeying rule (2b) and if they veered at the last moment we would change our minds and cross over, reverting to what ever version of the rule or rules led to the most pandemonium. I am sure the chaos will be continuing to this day on the corridors of the school. I wonder if this is how the game of Rugby started. As Robbie Burns once never said, "The best laid schemes o' mice and men and Shercliff School teachers....."

Anyway back to the plot.

In the third year I reached the dizzy heights of art monitor. This was because there were dozens of crayons to be sharpened and I was the only one with a pen knife despite the fact that on Coronation Day every boy in the city was given one, a solid lump of plastic with a flimsy blade - a disgrace to Sheffield tradition. What my dad would have described as bloody rammel! (Now there's a word you haven't heard for a while.) If I remember correctly the girls were given a pair of scissors instead of a knife because, well, because they were just girls!

My own knife was a proper pearl hafted knife which I sharpened on the step every week. It was so sharp in fact that I cut myself whilst sharpening a crayon and I was immediately sacked as art monitor and replaced by my mate Haggis. When he was instructed to appoint a friend to help him, guess who he chose. Me and my pen knife were only unemployed for half a day!

A passing phase around that time was that all the boys went around wearing a woolly Khaki army hat, known affectionately as a Rickie Hat. The Rickhill family just up the road owned two lorries which things had the habit of falling onto the back of. They were into wheeling and dealing and bought a job lot of these hats (probably from the Magnet) and sold them off for sixpence each to all the kids in the area.

The craze spread like wildfire and for several weeks the schoolyard must have looked like an army parade ground.

When I reached fourth year I was in Mr. Wilson's class, though I'm sure he never noticed. Classes were large and just like Dickie Valentine he appeared to pay more attention to the girls.

This fashion continued for quite a while then in 1954 it died as suddenly as it had come.

A new film with a memorable theme tune came out and overnight all the little "soljas" of the Sheffield 5 Regiment were transformed into miniature versions of Davy Crockett and went around with beaver skin hats singing "Born on a Mountain Top in Tennessee" (It could have been raccoon not beaver - I'm not a zoologist.) With the furry tail hanging down the back it didn't matter if your neck was weshed or not.

When I reached fourth year I was in Mr. Wilson's class, though I'm sure he never noticed. Classes were large and just like Dickie Valentine he appeared to pay more attention to the girls. He seemed to go through the motions of education, putting in just enough effort to get the day over, which seemed like an eternity to teacher and kids alike.

During a spelling lesson he once tried to teach us the golden rule "I before E except after C" but he said not one word about "When the sound is E." He then went on to say that there are some exceptions to the rule, which was just about as useful as saying there is no such rule at all.

When he gave us a test my superior logic told me that a vindictive sod like Wilson would never give us the straight-forward words, they must all be exceptions.

He couldn't understand why I broke all records by "achieving" none out of ten in the ensuing test. I am not in favour of modern day School Inspections but I do wonder how many of life's opportunities my generation has missed due to lack of effort and absence of accountability by the teaching staff of yester year. Either that or I am just thick and I don't feel thick.

Our junior school used to have a magnificent May Day celebration.

This was not the socialist-red flag-trade union-labour sort of May Day.

No, this was a Pretty Flowers- School Captain-May Queen-Train-Bearer

-May pole-songs- about-cool gales shall fan the glade-type of May Day. By way of preparation, for many weeks before, classes had to be re-scheduled, choirs had to practice, and maypole dancers had to be trained.

The whole event was always a tremendous success and put other schools in the area to shame. The head mistress Mrs. Battle Axe and her staff were immensely proud.

But it was marred by just one rather fundamental oversight. Whilst we were preparing for our extravaganza the other schools were preparing for the "Scholarship" exams.

The neighbouring school at Longley would typically get all the "A" class and half of the "B" class through the scholarship, whilst in my year only the top ten of the "A" class passed for grammar school. (I was positioned eleventh in the A class by the way!)

But never mind all that exam malarkey. We had a wonderful May Day.

In adult years when writing out a CV or attending job interviews where a degree is expected, I have often thought of emphasising the unquestionable success of our May Day event, but I feel that today's employers would somehow miss the significance. I know I did.

Incidentally, at Christmas when our education could have afforded a light relief, the opportunity was not seized with the same enthusiasm.

Instead of a proper nativity play, the teachers, still exhausted from their May Day efforts, did not attempt a proper nativity play as was the national tradition.

We just had a tableau. We got dressed up in the usual towels and blankets, (I was a shepherd of course) and whilst the choir sang, we just sort of stood there not moving. The excitement was breathtaking.

But again I digress.

I recall one day during a geography lesson, Mr. Wilson, just as an irrelevant aside, suddenly remembered that the scholarship exams were coming up soon and asked if we were ready and did we know what to expect and were we prepared. No we weren't, no we didn't and no we weren't!

He then wrote on the blackboard something like:-

$$\text{"}\Delta \, \partial \, \maltese \, \lozenge \, \square \, \Omega \, \infty\text{"}$$

He just shrugged, smirked as if to say "You lot have got no chance in the Scholarship exams!" and he carried on with the geography lesson.

saying that it said "TRICKLE" He then wrote,

"☐ ⚐ Δ"

and asked us what it said. Only one child, which happened to be me, put a hand up and said, (yes, yes, I know you are all in front of me here) that the answer, the secret password to a scholarship, a proper education and a proper school, was, "KIT"

Now at this point Mr. Wilson could have continued with an explanation. He could have panicked at our open mouthed reaction, re-scheduled his lesson, dished out some homework, given further examples, shown some concern for his future employment, or just resigned. But he did none of these things. There was another rather important thing he didn't do. He did not offer one single word of explanation of the conundrum he had put on the blackboard.

He just shrugged, smirked as if to say "You lot have got no chance in the Scholarship exams!" and he carried on with the geography lesson.

And this is the bastard who once called me lazy in front of the whole school.

Well Mr. Wilson, I have three things to say to you.

Firstly may I congratulate you on matching accurately the educational achievements of your pupils with the limited requirements of Sheffield's heavy industry in the nineteen fifties.

Secondly, there are thirty five people now in their mid sixties, still waiting to hear from you what "☐ ⚐ Δ" means.

I have had the courtesy to enlighten them in this humble book. If you had given them the password to a better education five decades ago their lives might have taken a different direction.

Thirdly, if when you depart this earth you reach the pearly gates and you don't know the required password entitling you to a better life, I hope at least that your years of purgatory are not made worse by the presence of Miss Morrissey and Mr. Dobbins.

I am not a bitter man.

Five Arches - end of an era

Parkwood Springs - view from Medders

Chapter Three
Shopping on 'Medder Street.'

So much for junior education or lack of. What of home life? One predominant memory is of three very hungry kids waiting at the window for Mam to come home from work. On Fridays she got paid and shopped on "Medder Street" before struggling home on the bus, late, dirty with factory grime and sagging under the weight of two massive shopping bags. When we saw her coming we would let the dog out to chase down the road and jump up and "fuss" her then we would meet her at the door shouting,

"Food Foood Fooooood Fooooooood."

But after a long hard day in the factory she never found this quite as entertaining as we did. Even so, the wait was worth it as Fridays brought special treats such as a quarter of sweets between the whole family, a bottle of Tizer or Dandelion and Burdock to be saved for Sunday dinner, and an Eccles cake. Sometimes there would be Booze Cake which must have been a Medder Street delicacy as I have never heard of it anywhere else. It had a sherry flavour and I was convinced it made me drunk when I had my one quarter ration.

I should explain here that my mother's way of sharing cake, orange or apple between three kids was to cut it into one half and two quarters. I don't think the nuns at her school in 1920 stretched to geometry. A far better method was the "Thee cut and I'll pick" system. One person, usually our Alan, would be given the job of cutting but was last to have his pick of the pieces.

Believe me; the pieces were so similar in size that our Norma and I took for ever making our choice. Nowadays it is claimed that this sharing method was invented by the Inuits for sharing out whale blubber but I know for a fact it was started by my Grandmother. How they got the idea from her I don't know because she never ventured near the Arctic Circle to my knowledge.

If the treat in question was an orange, we would often agree to roast it first on the open fire until the skin had black scorch marks on.

The demise of the planet due to open coal fires is entirely justified by the incredible flavour of roasted orange. It is a treat now lost to the world. Other treats at the time included tiger nuts, liquorice root and locust beans. These were all rock hard, dry and indigestible, needing so much chewing to develop sufficient saliva to extract the juices that there must have been a net loss of energy. Not so much a health food, more like an exercise. But even at that tender age these snacks gave us a feeling of curiosity for distant lands occupied by people whose cultures we could only imagine.

The writing of this book set me on a nostalgic mission and I recently tracked down a packet of tiger nuts. They taste just like the ones obtained in my childhood. In fact they taste like the very same ones which have been put aside and eaten fifty years later.

Us kids were not afraid of experimenting with foodstuffs. My older brother was the scientific one and my sister very imaginative, whereas I was either the audience or the guinea pig. One idea was to repeatedly eat the brown skin off rice pudding and then put it back on the stove top to form another skin. (Everyone knows that production of brown skin is the only purpose for rice pudding, which for that reason is the most unproductive of dishes.)

Another experiment, only tried once, was to make cheese by making milk go sour and draining the liquid off. (Yoghurt wasn't invented at the time.) Heaven knows where our parents were whilst this was going on.

Anyway we are still alive and we were convinced at the time that the fruit of our labour was delicious. I think we would have said so whatever the result.

By far the most successful of these ventures was dried apple rings. Get an apple, preferably a cooker, core it out, peel it and slice it into rings. Thread them on a string spaced out and hang them over a Yorkshire Range for several days. (It doesn't work over any other type of stove.) The guinea pig (me) was allowed the first taste and it was delicious, having a beautiful, mature after-taste. Having survived and declared the experiment a success my elder siblings scoffed the lot saying it was their idea/their string/their apple etc. I should have pretended to be sick and offered to get rid of it.

A more common treat which will be familiar to readers who are still with me, was raw sticks of rhubarb, peeled if you are a wimp, and dipped into sugar in a cone made from the Sheffield Star. (My wife says they used saucers. They were posh on their street. And anyway they didn't get The Star in Liverpool). We pretended to like it but, despite the sugar when we chewed the stalks, our little faces were fit to win a gurning competition. Sometimes we got our own tea ready and the favourite - always on a Wednesday for reasons unknown - was hash, which Mam had made the day before. Usually my mam would leave a hurriedly written note, sometimes written on the blank "Latest" column torn from The Star, but more often if this was over-stamped with some dramatic late news, she would use the flap of an old envelope.

The note would tell us to help ourselves to hash, but her capital 'H' always looked like an 'N' and hash is affectionately known as "Nash" amongst us siblings to this day. It was the only meal of the week where extra portions were available and when still hungry we were not instructed to "Fill up wi bread!" In fact the Nash usually stretched to the next day, though a bit thinner with water and an Oxo added.

It usually contained dumplings, the purpose of which was to soak up loads of Henderson's Relish.

By chance, on the very day that I relate this tale I have just packed an emergency parcel of three bottles of Henderson's for my sister in Brighton. The bloke at work in our keep-old-boxes-and-bubble-wrap-for-packing-Henderson's-Relish department, abandoned all other duties and treated the matter with the importance and urgency which only Henderson's Relish deserves. He must be a true Dee Dah. (i.e. a Sheffielder as in "naah den dee, what dah dooin" etc.)

An occasional alternative to hash was "Bacon Booan Soup." It contained ham bones, rice, lentils and Oxo, was very plentiful, very wholesome and very, very salty but it never did us any harm. (Stops writing to take a blood pressure tablet.) One day the school dinners van didn't arrive because of snow. (Old fogies will recollect that snow was eighteen feet deep for ten months every year when it wasn't sun-shining fit to melt the pavement for the other ten months of summer.) I used to sit with Chris Smith for dinner and I took him to our house

If we were still hungry after a meal my mam's favourite expression was "Fill up wi' bread." and we would help ourselves to that Shepherd delicacy "bread and jam wi' butter underneath."

where my dad, being on shifts at the time, was at home. He served up a big portion each of bacon booan soup with a big slice of crusty bread. After three basins full the pair of us sat bloated at school all afternoon whilst our classmates couldn't concentrate on anything but their hunger.

We had chips for tea quite often considering that we didn't have a chip pan. The chips were shallow fried one side at a time in a frying pan and served to each person in turn with a fifteen minute gap between.

After I had watched the others devouring their chips I was starving hungry and by the time I got mine they had got hungry again.

Eventually this problem was overcome when us kids negotiated a complex chip lending agreement of which the mafia itself would have been proud.

My mam was never out of the kitchen but always at supper time us kids would ask for something a bit more substantial than biscuits or bread and my mam would reply with one of her favourite expressions.

"Yer want summat for every meal yo."

(The word "yo" is the plural of "you" in Sheffield 5 terminology though it is not to be found in the many available books on Yorkshire dialect)

If we were still hungry after a meal my mam's favourite expression was "Fill up wi' bread." and we would help ourselves to that Shepherd delicacy "bread and jam wi' butter underneath."

Another of our favourites was bread and butter with sugar on. Delicious but not found in Government health guides. (Stops writing to take diabetes tablets.)

Despite the fact that fattening food was plentiful there were always a few kids in school who were obviously underprivileged even when measured against the very modest standard which prevailed. Sometimes these kids would be whisked away for a spell at Fairthorn Lodge convalescent home, from which they would reappear fitter, cleaner, happier, fatter and almost unrecognisable, with necks weshed.

Presumably their needs had been recognised by the School Nurse who came round weighing and measuring everybody and looking for nits. I always wondered what she was for and why she wanted the nits.

Another frequent part of our diet was bread cakes with dripping.

My mam always enthused about the jellified brown stuff at the bottom of the dripping, which she referred to as 'Gravy Bottoms.' She used to say it was all the goodness out of the dripping, (implying that the rest was badness?) and when spread on top of the dripping on a bread cake with a liberal sprinkling of salt, it became what I referred to in my tender years as "Cakey Goodness."

In the absence of dripping we were known to use lard. I won't pretend it was very nice but it was OK with a layer of salt on top and it didn't do me any harm. (Pauses again to take cholesterol tablet.)

I cannot leave the subject of food without further mention of my mother's home made bread cakes.

It is every autobiographer's duty to mention his mam's bread cakes. She had no time for weight scales and measured everything by experienced guesswork, a handful here, a pinch there, and put it in the Yorkshire Range oven for which the temperature setting was measured in lumps of coal and position of a damper.

Cooking was timed on an old Westminster Chimes eight day clock which was wound up every twelve days.

I would like to announce to my dear readers here and now that my mam's bread cakes were the most consistent, succulent, soft and delicious bread cakes ever to grace Sheffield. That is what I would like to announce to my dear readers. Unfortunately they were crap!

We were well served by shops just up Teynham Road. In the grocers, Roy Smith, commonly known as Rob Roy, was exactly like Arkwright on Open All Hours. He had a habit of shouting out "Come on you lucky people!" in street hawker fashion, to no one's amusement. Fans of Maggie Thatcher would have you believe that corner shop keepers were working class but in reality they were considered very well off in those pre-supermarket days. Behind his high wall topped with broken glass Rob Roy kept a magnificent Humber Super Snipe. I wanted it then and I want it now.

Housewives used to moan at him for charging a penny or two more than town prices but he knew, and they knew, that they had neither the bus fare nor the time to go to town every day.

Across the road was the chip shop and greengrocers, both owned by the Parkin family. They too were rich and the daughter was rumoured to have a real horse. Their compound didn't need broken glass on top of the wall. Inside was a large Alsatian which barked its head off every time someone passed by from the bus stop, which happened to approximately ten people every fifteen minutes between five am. and twelve pm. On the gate was emblazoned an unnecessary sign, obviously prepared by the daughter of the family, which was enough to terrify the life out of any potential potato thief. It read,

"PLEASE BEWARE OF OUR BRUCE PLEASE."

Before they built the Five Arches pub and the paper shop, the land at Teynham Road was our playing field and the side wall of the chip shop was an excellent substitute for a sight screen, a wicket keeper and several silly mid whatevers. (I never quite got the hang of cricket.) In front of the wall we erected a set of cricket stumps which we knocked in with my dad's lump hammer. Every time I missed the hard "corky" ball, which was every time Gus bowled at me, it hit the wall with a resounding crash which echoed through the hallowed premises of the chippie.

Eventually Mr. Parkin came out, played hell and took the hammer, presuming we had been hammering the wall. He made some comment about telling the police and as he retreated I said that the next policeman to come around would be sent by me, to arrest him for stealing my dad's hammer. This was the first time in my life I had ever spoken so boldly to an adult and I was amazed when he thought better of it and gave me back the hammer. He should have stood his ground because I have been defiant in the face of authority ever since.

The field was the centre of our universe and numerous kids would kick a ball around or play cricket on there.

On occasions a bloke from one of the private houses up Herries Road would come out with a big piston engined aeroplane which he would fly in circles on a long wire. No radio control in the fifties, just wire. We would lie down in the grass at the edge of the circular flight path and watch in

Every chicken knows its place in society without having to peck or be pecked very often. A similar rule applies to the game of conkers.

amazement until one day the plane suddenly dived down and hit a lad from Adkins Road smack on the forehead with propeller at full revs, throwing blood everywhere.

The bloke never brought the plane out again and the lad still had the scar up to leaving senior school.

Another major aspect of a schoolboy's life was fighting. Not that fighting was commonplace, it was just very significant.

You will be well aware of the pecking order which takes place amongst farmyard chickens. Every chicken knows its place in society without having to peck or be pecked very often.

A similar rule applies to the game of conkers, whereby even a virgin conker could become a "conker 100" just by beating one "conker 99" and so it was with fighting. Everyone knew their position in the hierarchy without having to prove it too often and even when a fight occurred it was usually fair and ethical although my dad always advised me, if outnumbered or losing to a bigger boy, to "Get Timpsons in." (Timpsons was the big shoe shop of the day, but you already know that surely.) Another of his favourite pieces of advice, though not meant quite so seriously, was "If you can't feight, wear a big hat!"

I was one of the smallest in my age group and the only way to survive without being bullied for life was to keep face and fight back determinedly when necessary. I didn't want to, but I had to. In this way, and aided by my scruffy appearance, I maintained quite a high position in the hierarchy considering my size, but it was not without dire consequences on occasions. I was reminded of this when I was reunited with my old mate Haggis on his 50th birthday. It did not take him long to start admonishing me with a question that had burned within him ever since school days. "Graham, what the hell were you doing trying to fight Mick Slade. NOBODY fights Mick Slade!"

This conversation with Haggis inspired the following poem which sums up the whole fighting issue as applied back then.

The Day I Fought Mick Slade

We didn't learn much at our school.
It were a waste of time
A bit of spelling here and there, a
sum, and the odd rhyme
But one thing's firmly fixed in mind, a
lesson that won't fade
You absolutely, definitely, do not,
fight Mick Slade

Our ethics then were based upon
the heroes of the west.
Roy Rodgers, the Lone Ranger, Tex
Ritter and the rest
Would never hit below the belt or
bite or scratch or kick
P'raps Mick hadn't seen them films,
or p'raps Mick was just thick!

He didn't know his scripture, at
hist'ry he'd no chance
He didn't join the choir or do the
maypole dance
He wasn't cheeky or mischievous,
not a naughty lad
No-he was nasty, bitter, evil, hard
and bad!
But one thing he excelled at, he
could apply his brain
To causing fear and anguish and
excruciating pain

I don't recall the argument, don't
remember a discussion

(My lack of recollection could be due
to the concussion)
I thought of going to fetch our kid, a
bigger, older lad,
But I thought that Mick might flatten
him then kill my Mam and Dad

I don't know what the fight was for,
what I wanted to achieve
Something about dignity and honour
I believe
But dignity and honour aren't easy
to sustain
When you're lying in a battered heap
and groaning out with pain

It started with a little shove, then
they packed around like leeches
Shouting Feight, Feight, Feight,
Feight, Feight, Feight, Feight
And that was just the teachers!
They formed a circle round us in
accordance with the rules
I'm sure that hundreds must have
come from other nearby schools
To witness the demise of a
masochist, first grade
In combat with a solid block of
granite called Mick Slade

Well I thumped and punched and
pummelled till my knuckle bones
were bare

42

Get Thi Neck Weshed

And in the end Mick Slade began to notice I was there,
Which was bad news for both of us, cos then, he lost his cool
And he began to growl and grunt and curse and spit and drool

The fight was quickly over. I lost in the first round.
A bloody red pulsating lump of flesh upon the ground
But all that didn't matter. My street cred was intact
And schoolgirls love an underdog, that's a well-known fact
They like boys to be tender. It makes their little hearts melt
And for several weeks thereafter, tender's how I felt

As time went by my life improved. Mick Slade came nowhere near
I didn't meet him after that. The coast, as they say, was clear
The fight was our last contact. It was the final curtain
Our paths have never crossed again. (Cos I make bloody certain)

But to this day when I dine out the fight still comes to mind
I look around to see if he is sitting there behind

And when the waiter hovers as the bill is being paid
I give him such a useful tip.
"Don't ever fight Mick Slade!"

Readers might well assume from the above that Mick Slade was a hard case. Your reason for thinking that is because you never met Barry Harker. Barry was a real villain of the piece who made Mick Slade look like a lovable little cherub.

When Harker approached, everyone including me, in fact everyone led by me, melted away out of sight. As number one school bully he was actually quite ineffective because he could rarely find anybody to bash. He would often swagger through the playground surrounded by a vacuum. He must have been a very frustrated and lonely boy. In fact he must have often wondered if he had made a mistake and turned up at school during the six week holiday.

The last I heard of Barry was a report in The Star some years later, saying that he had been jailed for having a gun under the seat in his car. But this must surely have been a mistake. Whereas it was probably his gun, I very much doubt that it was his car.

Get Thi Neck Weshed

Where violence is concerned I would never have taken part in bullying as I had enough trouble with fights started by other people. However, in these enlightened times we recognise that bullying can exist in the form of social exclusion and psychological aggression, in which case I might have to plead guilty.

One girl in our class, not called Beryl, came from a rather inadequate family. She must have been quite intelligent because she was in the top half of the A class, yet nobody ever heard her speak or interacted with her. She had dirty hair and was always dressed in old clothes that didn't quite fit. I never checked, but I don't think it likely that she had her neck weshed by a loving mum.

She was a total outcast from the class. Me and Gus invented the fact that she was always producing farts which wreaked total devastation on the landscape, turned every unwary victim into a dark green smouldering heap and was a potential source of military power. We spent quite a few playtimes keeping our distance and ducking for cover when she turned her back towards us. To be fair to myself, the whole situation was not vindictive but was driven by a weird sense of humour which Gus and I shared, with no intention to hurt or offend Beryl. In fact she is probably unaware to this day of our private joke and we never encouraged anyone else to join in.

At some point later I remember Beryl was absent for the day and a forward thinking lady teacher took the opportunity to say to the class that Beryl didn't seem to have any friends and it might be an idea if some of the girls tried to include her a bit more. One or two of them did, and me and Gus, rather shamefully, decided to find another way to entertain ourselves at playtime.

I wonder what kind of life Beryl has had. I certainly hope that I have not influenced it in any negative way. Aren't boys horrible.

A similar situation occurred with a girl in the year above us who I will call Kilner because she wasn't called that. She too was a bit of an outcast but rougher and tougher than Beryl.

It was an established fact that if you were careless enough to touch Kilner you would suffer from the dreaded Kilner Touch. This was never defined clearly but to compare it with a kind of plague or leprosy was to

I wonder what happened to Kilner later in life. It would be lovely if she met up with Beryl, formed a loving relationship and opened a successful business advising schools how to recognise and counteract the effects of evil little brats like me.

seriously understate the case. As time went by the situation worsened and anyone who touched anyone who touched anyone who touched anyone who had the Kilner Touch would themselves have the Kilner Touch. Some people who had the Kilner Touch did the right thing and deliberately avoided touching their friends. Others, once infected, went around the playground with new-found powers threatening to infect others who didn't do their bidding. A few of them even extracted payment for not infecting others and the payment was placed for collection without human contact, a bit like the provisions left out for the occupants of the Plague village of Eyam.

I wonder what happened to Kilner later in life. It would be lovely if she met up with Beryl, formed a loving relationship and opened a successful business advising schools how to recognise and counteract the effects of evil little brats like me.

To the dismay of the kids and the delight of the adults, there came the day when the Five Arches pub was built, on what we regarded as "our" playing field.

On the day it opened, the car park was full of chauffeur driven limousines and a uniformed doorman with peak cap showed everyone in. I watched in disbelief, thinking what a posh, up and coming area I lived in, never considering for a moment that the arrangements were just for the ceremonial opening. The posh officials soon went away but the pub retained a very strict dress code for years after. If you didn't wear a flat cap you didn't go in.

There were a few interesting characters amongst the pub regulars.

One lady was known as Leg O'er Lil but my dad would never elaborate on the reason.

A young man not called Crooksie, like several locals, earned his living from dodgy scrap deals and lived his life on the fringes of the law.

He needed a good income to support a rapidly growing family. Once when his mate pulled his leg, saying,

"People will be talking about you-having five kids in six years"

Crooksie replied quite indignantly,

"Well, I can't help it, I was doing time last year otherwise it would have been six."

Another five Arches regular not called Les Holland, would entertain everyone in the concert room on a Saturday night with his song about "Tha's been out wi' pot mo' Nellie all day" - a classic which never quite reached the top twenty.

This was before the days of betting shops and Les's popularity led him to do a roaring trade at lunch times in the car park taking bets, but occasionally he would have a customer he didn't bargain for. The police would turn up, perhaps in an old car or dressed as bread delivery men, and take Les away. This would all be taken in good spirit and when he had been nicked too often and the fines got more expensive it would be mutually agreed that it was his son's turn and their Mick would be fetched out of the pub to take the rap. One day there was a big race and the wrong horse won, or lost or whatever, and Les couldn't pay anybody out. One might have expected a missing person's report in The Star or at least an unexplained pool of blood in the Five Arches toilets but Les was quite well respected and the punters of Parson Cross and Shercliff were quite forgiving under the circumstances. However he did the honourable thing and resigned his bookieship. The punters had to revert to the alternative bookie who sat in his car up the hill on Pollard Crescent outside the home of a young blind boy called David Blunkett. You might have heard of him.

But time moves on and fings ain't wot they used to be. Since those far off days, betting shops have sprouted up on every corner and now even these are under threat as you can put your money on a horse by logging on to the internet. And just to remind me how times change, as I passed by Herries Road the other day, a great big machine resembling a preying mantis cross-bred with a dinosaur stood devouring the Five Arches pub lump by lump. I am reminded of the words from that old song our Folk Group sometimes sing. "They're tearing down buildings I once watched them build. It's time, just time."

On the bright side, the site is returned to its original form, a field of sanctuary, an uncluttered area ideal for the next generation of little Shercliff kids to spend their leisure time.

What a shame it is completely surrounded by an impenetrable eight foot fence.

During holidays us kids fended for ourselves all day and quite often my mam would leave some money and a note, on a triangular envelope flap of course, telling us to go to't Stooers. (Now called the Co-op) for something to eat. Even a little brat like me could see the inefficiency of making customers queue at the "Tea" side for half the order then move over to the queue on the "Bacon" side for the rest.

Typically the Co-op management could never grasp this point.

Fortunately, unless milk cheques were on the order, us kids rarely had to join the third queue at the office window where the grown up business of Divi was dealt with.

Further delay resulted from the fact that the assistants chatted to each other for hours, the long queue being totally invisible to them. Frequently a couple of them would disappear upstairs for a skive, but thanks to my inventive brother we were able to express our disapproval. The Co-op was 100 yards due south of our house and when a couple of white coated Co-op assistants appeared with a fag at the upstairs window we would take the big mirror off our wall and reflect a broad beam of sunlight straight at them. (This was during the ten months of constant sun, not the ten months per year when the snow was up to the wall tops. But if you told that to the kids of today they wouldn't believe you!)

Nobody ever complained to Mam about the mirror trick - perhaps they felt guilty about their unofficial fag breaks.

Or perhaps they knew that my uncle George was president of the Co-op. True to its principles the Co-op appointed its president by shareholder votes and every so often the Shepherd kids would be given leaflets to distribute around the streets of Parsons Cross, ten miles across the city from where George worked. Our campaigns were successful and every so often when on the way from an important meeting he would stop at our house in a chauffeur driven Rolls Royce. My mother would try to insist that he bring the chauffeur in for a cuppa but George would refuse,

On one occasion our Norma kidded me into asking the butcher to "put it on't strap for Mrs. Shepherd." much to the amusement of the butcher and all the women in the shop,

saying that the bloke was getting paid overtime and was quite happy sitting there. Despite these moments of grandeur most of George's days were spent in quite humble circumstances cutting up meat in his Co-op butchers shop up Handsworth.

On one occasion my mam went up to the Stooers and our Norma tied a note to our Gyp's collar and let him out of the back door.

He was obsessed with my mam and took off across Herries Road over the Zebra crossing, (an act for which he was world famous throughout Herries Road) and straight to mam who was just getting served on the "tea side". She retrieved the note, read it and to the amusement of all, calmly said to the assistant

"Oh-and a tin of Andrews Liver salts please." Our Gyp got a standing ovation. No Yorkshire book of reminiscence is complete without the author declaring that he still remembers his mother's divi number, so never let it be said that my book contains a serious omission. It was 15681. Any Co-op accountants reading this might like to check if there is any unclaimed divi which has been accumulating interest for the past 50 years. They must have got spare money from somewhere - they have acquired their own bank since I was a lad.

Sometimes in school holidays we would be instructed in writing, on a triangular envelope flap, to buy liver or sausage for dinner from the butchers. We didn't need money for this. We just had to say politely "Would you book it please for Mrs. Shepherd." Thanks to my mam's incredible ability to budget, this small sum, outstanding until Saturday morning, was as close as our family ever came to debt.

Instead of the "book it please" routine, on one occasion our Norma kidded me into asking the butcher to "put it on't strap for Mrs. Shepherd." much to the amusement of the butcher and all the women in the shop, but to my acute embarrassment.

I will get you back for that one day Norma.

Chapter Four
A sawn off mongrel named Gyp

Our Gyp. Total value 7/6d (collar included)

I have made mention already of our dog. He was a sort of sawn off mongrel version of a border collie, modelled after grandma's Mick. His name was Gyp. In my head I invented the secret posh pedigree name, Rip Gyp Jilkner. But needless to say I never called that name out in the street. Let's face it, he only answered to Gyp when he felt inclined or when his dish was rattled at the same time. Incidentally, does anyone know why people used to put lumps of yellow sulphur in dog's water bowls in the fifties? Perhaps for the same reason that our Alan was made to eat brimstone and treacle and on some occasions soot from the fire back, stirred in water. It never cured his boils and the sulphur did nothing for the dog and nothing for any of us, especially when our Alan set fire to some over the gas stove and we all had to go outside until the poisonous yellow fumes had gone away.

But I digress. When we first got Gyp we made grand preparations. My dad got a big roll of wire netting, presumably bought from the Magnet, and we built a fence all around the substantial garden, and finished it off with a big wooden gate. The first time we let Gyp loose he ran twice round the garden then leapt over the fence and disappeared.

On one occasion in Dicko's Wood, Gyp was attacked by a free roaming Alsatian and was pinned to the ground by the throat, yelping in terror. In desperation I jumped astride the Alsatian, grasped it between my knees and lashed it repeatedly with a heavy chain dog lead but it didn't even notice my presence so I changed my tactics, found a stick, forced it into the dog's mouth and levered its jaws apart.

Gyp was released and the Alsatian stood there blinking in confusion, wondering why a flavoursome collie dog should suddenly taste like a dry stick. The fur around Gyp's neck was so thick that no blood was spilled but he was covered in alstian spit and had to have his annual bath a bit early.

One of Gyp's worst habits emerged whenever I took him in open spaces, especially "daan't medders" more politely known as Parkwood Springs. He would run off quite a distance and then, either in response to a call (rarely) or of his own volition (frequently) he would come dashing back like a bullet from a gun. He didn't slow down at all on arrival but if I moved left he would curve the same way and knock me flying. If I moved right three times in succession so would he, and if I stood still he would keep straight on and collide with me.

On one occasion I even tried standing still with legs apart but he still managed somehow to hit both legs and flatten me.

I still think about all this with great sympathy whenever I watch a goalkeeper taking a penalty, knowing that which ever way he jumps will be the wrong way.

Nevertheless Rip Gyp Jilkner was a starry dog. And so he should be. He cost us seven and sixpence, collar included.

Other pets came and went in the Shepherd household. One of the cats we had was a sleek black creature called "Our Evil" All of his behaviour was evil but his name was chosen for his unprovoked attacks upon the forearm, growling like a dog, clutching on with front claws, and kicking against the arteries with his back feet, whilst simultaneously chewing the wrist with needle-like teeth, ears flattened back like a lion with a gazelle. We presumed he was playing. I wouldn't like to see him get nasty. Fortunately we had some respite from all this because Our Evil would spend about four days with us then disappear for the same length of time. My dad reckoned that it was not really our cat and somewhere there was another family who thought it was theirs. This was entirely feasible considering that he was an adopted stray.

The way that Our Evil was obtained would be considered bizarre by today's standards. Me and my pal Gus were playing in Scraify (Scraith Wood) when we saw Our Evil stuck up a big mature sycamore tree. We left him to come down by himself but he was still there next day so we contacted the RSPCA.

The two grey haired gentlemen who attended looked older than the tree and had no intention of climbing it, so I volunteered. Without so much as a duplicated risk assessment or permission from my next of kin they authorised me to climb a tree that even a cat couldn't get down. I went up about 30 feet, crawled snake-like along the branch and grabbed the cat. To return I needed the same four limbs I had used to get up there and one was occupied with the cat, so they held out a blanket below and I let the cat drop.

Down he sailed, using up several of his nine lives as he crashed through the lighter twigs and missed all the harder branches whilst demonstrating the feline knack of turning feet downward.

Not only did he miss the branches, (yes, you're probably ahead of me here) he missed the blanket as well! He landed with a splat beside the aghast RSPCA men.

Not only did Our Evil survive, miraculously so did I. And so did the jobs of the RSPCA men.

Our Evil. Pretending to be cuddly whilst savaging Norma's throat (Norma camouflaged against the brick wall.)

Get Thi Neck Weshed

When I volunteered to take the cat home the RSPCA men just said OK
without any thought of rules and regulations, the cat's previous owners
or my parents' opinion on the matter. It seems that in those days the only
qualification to be an RSPCA man was the ability to hold out a blanket
without getting it spoiled by a falling cat.

Other cats came and went in the Shepherd household. A ginger one we
had was obtained after Norma and I sat on the stairs on strike, refusing to
go to bed until my dad agreed. This risky business was carefully planned
and we waited until my dad had been to the pub before we took on such
an act of defiance. Tact, manipulation and humour won the day and we
got the cat.

Unfortunately the poor thing had to be put down when a neighbour, Old
Bilton, threw a rock at it and broke its jaw. This was a motiveless crime as
there was nothing in his garden worth protecting from cats except uneven
lumps of grass sod.

The sight of the cat running around in confusion with its bottom jaw at
right angles to its face is as clear to me now as the day it occurred and
my hatred of Old Bilton is as strong as ever, the evil old git. (And yes,
Bilton was his real name Why should I shield the old sod?)

For his remaining years Old Bilton had no peace on this earth because
his life was plagued by mysterious strange, unexplained annoying noises
and incidents around his house, garden and even in his kitchen when the
back door was open. But he was never able to find out who or what was
responsible. Perhaps it was poltergeists.

This made his later years so miserable that when his time on earth was
over it was probably a relief to spend eternity in the company of Mr.
Wilson, Miss Morrissey etc. (I hope you have been listening.) Heaven
knows Old Bilton was such a miserable old sod when he was on this
earth that eternal fire and brimstone is probably a light relief for him. I do
hope so. I am not a vindictive man.

Me and Norma made a hobby of observing other cats around the area.
One visitor to our garden was called Cushion Face because, well,
because it had a cushion for a face. Another we named "That Bear"
because it was a bear. Another was in the habit of saying "Ang Gang Grrr"
when approached, to our great fear and amusement, so that became its

name. Another cat appeared on our front garden and on three or four occasions, looked up at us and said in gurgling tones,
"Can you credit it?"
I am sure my dear readers will indeed not credit it but I swear to you that this is a clear recollection from my tender years. However the distant memory may have been reinforced by reminiscences with my sister and if you met her she would easily convince you that a cat could not only speak but could quote the entire works of Shakespeare. Come to think of it she would persuade the cat to prove it.
Our Evil was not the only stray we adopted. My mate Dicteen's dad was a policeman and one day they arrested a budgie for vagrancy, flying without a licence or something.
They took it into custody in Hammerton Road nick but the bars being too wide to contain a budgie they quickly looked for the first mug they could find and I ended up with it.
Whereas most budgies just sit on a perch waiting to die, this one was full of personality and was absolutely barmy. It would fly around, land on your shoulder and chirp in your ear as though telling you secrets until you were lulled into a sense of false security then it would bite your ear lobe and hang on for dear life.
If you tried to read the paper it would land on the top edge and bite off hundreds of little triangular pieces whilst shrieking its head off. It would land on the "Cornish" (which people at Dore call a mantelpiece), pick up all the money which was laid out awaiting various transactions, and throw the coins down one by one. It would then do the same with my dad's fags and matches, then the spills, dad's arm bands, mam's hair net, grips, those things that women grasped their hair with to make waves but I can't remember the name of, the rent book, the gas bill, everything in the category of tranklements, and eventually trying to shoulder the chrome ornaments off the edge and into the tiled hearth. (A pair of chrome ornaments was obligatory on every council house Cornish.) If we tried to defend the ornaments with a prodding finger the crazy bird was not beyond biting and hanging on like a terrier even when shaken violently. Its most endearing habit, along with its yellow and green colouring, gave rise to its name, Lettuceface. (I have changed many names in this book to

One of the birds, aptly named Squawker, learned to imitate sparrows but much louder and also woke up before most Parson Cross dwellers.

avoid embarrassment but Lettuceface deserves to be embarrassed.) When presented with a wet lettuce leaf she would go completely nuts, squawking her head off, rolling, rubbing, tearing, nibbling and tossing it around for ages to the immense amusement and a standing ovation from the gathering crowd of incredulous onlookers.

One day I found an egg in the bottom of Lettuceface's cage. This prompted my dad to put the word out in the Magnet for a male bird. (I will refrain from the "budgie going cheep" joke and spare you the one about buying it on Higher Perches). He set up a breeding cage by putting a finer mesh on an old rabbit hutch of mine. Lettuce Face was mother to twenty or thirty babies in her time and started my dad on a major hobby which lasted for many years.

One day me and my mates were playing near the allotments in Dicko's Wood when we saw an old man taking a shed down so we told my dad and he went and offered him £4 for it. We brought it home on my trolley, (Are they now called go-karts or is that out of date too?) and set it up as a proper aviary. It survived for another twenty five years. We kept patching it up until in the end I don't think any of the original remained, still, not bad for four quid.

The hut went from strength to strength and was eventually extended with an outdoor aviary. Unfortunately one of the birds, aptly named Squawker, learned to imitate sparrows but much louder and also woke up before most Parson Cross dwellers. A neighbour complained to the council and my dad's major crime was revealed. He had not obtained planning permission for the garden shed. (I can hardly contain my shame to this day.) The outcome was that he had to apply for retrospective planning permission, which was refused because the hut had a sloping roof instead of an apex. We had to go to great lengths to make the roof conform to the required shape. Now, my dear reader, you get the opportunity to guess whether the new roof caused the stupid budgie to

On one occasion we were having Sunday tea and my dad told me that the day before he had found mice living in the corner of the budgie shed.

shut up and stop imitating amplified sparrows or lie in a little longer in the mornings. Eventually my dad got fed up of the bird himself and took to walking out of the aviary down to the house with it on his shoulder in the hope that it would fly away, but it never did.

Logic was not invented in those days and a house with one or two pet budgies and sixty more up the garden was not really the place for cats. Understandably there was the occasional disaster and I recall one of the birds being attacked by Our Evil. (It wasn't Lettuceface or the cat would have been killed outright.)

The poor bird had seed coming out of a one inch tear in its throat where its crop had been ripped open. For a three inch long budgie a one inch tear is a big tear.

My dad's response was to take it to one of his budgie mates who proceeded to sew its throat up with needle and thread. After that it was fine, lived for ages and fathered to a few offspring.

Other birds were less fortunate. When they became injured or terminally ill they would be unceremoniously put into a brown paper bag which was then placed over the kitchen gas tap to put them out of their misery.

On one occasion we were having Sunday tea and my dad told me that the day before he had found mice living in the corner of the budgie shed. What's more, the little devils had taken a new born baby budgie from its nest box into their own nest.

Fortunately he found it just in time and the baby, still alive, was replaced under mummy bird along with its brothers and sisters, who were still in their eggs.

Later on half way through the tinned pears and Carnation Milk I suddenly said "Dad, are you sure it was a baby budgie?" We ran up to the shed and pushed the complaining mummy bird aside to reveal three eggs and one little pink new born baby mouse. I took the mickey out of my dad for months after, imagining the mouse sitting upright on its perch, talking to itself in the mirror and squawking "WHO'S AN UGLY BOY THEN?"

Get Thi Neck Weshed

At one time we had a mouse of our own, a pure albino with pink eyes. It escaped one day and ran straight out of the back door and under the "coil oil" door through a gap that you would hardly get a sheet of paper through.

Every delivery of coal varied tremendously and on this occasion it was mostly pieces as big as house bricks, with hundreds of tunnels and spaces between the precariously balanced lumps. It must have been heaven for a fugitive mouse, though it could not have derived much comfort from its lack of camouflage. It certainly didn't want to be caught and for weeks we had many fleeting glimpses of the gradually greying creature but he was too quick for us.

Worst of all we were in constant fear of an avalanche with the mouse somewhere underneath so us kids had to fetch the coal in which we hand picked from the top very carefully, not trusting my dad in there with his big shovel. I think my dad was milking the situation a bit but eventually the mouse was caught again before the next coal delivery.

My dad was usually tired out and needed to rest his back when he got home from work, and would often fall asleep on the hearthrug with the newspaper over his face, a trait which according to our lass must be hereditary. He was not always well and on one occasion, after a working life bent over grinding machines, I remember him fully encased in plaster for several months looking like a tortoise.

Us kids thought this was great and wrote messages and drew pictures all over him. I think he was embarrassed about the graffiti when he went back to the hospital to have the plaster sawn off, but for the nurses and for us kids it was jolly good fun.

It has to be said that my mam and dad were not expert at bringing up children. I remember on one occasion I dreamed or imagined that a man was on the landing outside my bedroom door and I was terrified.

My dad's response, just for a joke, was to put his coat and hat on the banister post that night to look like the man I had complained of. I don't think that Doctor Spock's famous book was around at the time otherwise dad would have been locked up.

Anyway I don't remember it upsetting me much. Having said that, I am still moaning on about it all these years later.

On one occasion me and Norma were sent away for the week end to some casual acquaintance of my parents. They lived in the old Water Works cottages below Rivelin Dam. We had never met them before and felt totally out of place with these strangers, having no idea why we were there but somebody must have thought it was a good plan for us to be in the countryside for the weekend. I think they had children of our age but if so, we bonded so closely that I can't even swear that they existed.

In a similar way, at a very young and sensitive age I was sent away to stay with a young couple at a place called Sunnyside near Rotherham. They had a close relationship with me in that they were casual friends of a lady who used to drink in the Bull and Mouth on Castlegate with the people next door to us. Well I suppose that is a good enough reason to pass your treasured offspring into the hands of complete strangers for the week end. They had no children and I was quite a shy boy at the time so the conversation must have been very strained. On the Saturday morning the bloke took me to work with him. He was the driver of a steam shunter at the local pit and I was treated to a ride on the footplate, which made the whole weekend seem a lot better. But the incident had its moment of drama. As I leaned out from the footplate to look ahead I was suddenly yanked back just before the engine went under a narrow stone bridge which would have smashed my head in. I wonder to this day how my parents could just pack me off with these people who, for all they knew could have sold me into slavery or eaten me for breakfast.

Just to make a comparison, at the time of writing I am in the process of becoming an adoptive grandparent and we do feel quite frustrated by the delays whilst the powers that be conduct their police checks, ask for a written reference for a little dog and scrutinise the credentials and medical records of all the prospective parents. Compare this with my own childhood. Babysitted by a ten year old all summer, babysitting myself at the age of eleven and roaming Rivelin ponds in the dark with my young charges, of which more later, being farmed out to strangers whose motives and credentials were totally unknown to my parents. All this makes me appreciate how lucky I was to survive without some serious mishap occurring.

The difference is that was then. This is now!

Chapter Five
A typical Sheffield 5 dad

My dad was typical of Sheffield 5 dads in that he was the ultimate deterrent, with which mam would threaten us if we seriously misbehaved. When he was angry he would threaten to take his belt off to us and sometimes he would say "Tha'll get buckle end of this belt in a minute!" I was terrified of this and it is only now, as I recall past times, that I realise he never actually laid a finger, let alone a belt buckle on me. It is an unfortunate fact that fathers in those days believed it their duty to maintain an emotional distance from their children and an element of fear was regarded as necessary for a good disciplined upbringing.

In his crude way my dad had a simple sense of right and wrong and to express this he had a word of his own.

At the slightest suggestion of treating someone wrongly he would say "Nay, that's not fairation." This was the limit of his ability to teach ethics to his children, but in some ways it was enough. I am proud to say that the three of us have grown up with a strong sense of "fairation." What is more, my dad's legacy has been passed down to his six grandchildren. On most occasions my dad was quite jovial and was renowned for telling old jokes or singing funny songs. We loved to get him going when he'd had a drink. His favourite song "Bruvver Silvest"entered the repertoire of the folk group I played with, (Deepcar Folk) and has helped to make us famous for yards around.

Like everyone else we knew, my dad was working class and proud of it. Much of this pride was due to him being a "producer" and any non-producers were treated with disgust. The epitome of a non producer was our insurance man but this didn't stop mam or dad asking his advice if there were any queries on gas bills, rent books or similar. He was the only educated person to come near the house and not only did his shirt have a collar attached, it also sported a tie which gave him a real air of importance. Unfortunately his bicycle clips didn't contribute much at all to his otherwise sophisticated image.

My dad had a withered right arm which was permanently bent and looked like bone with skin stretched over it and he had a line of neat scars on his arm, shoulder and chest where I think glands had been removed. According to family legend he used to be bathed in a pint pot when he was a baby (Have you noticed how I am getting adept at this autobiography stuff? I am remembering things that occurred before I was born.) One family friend used to say every time she saw him, "He's not here for long, he'll soon be a lovely little angel" She was not a very tactful lady and not a very good fortune teller either. For one thing she was sixty nine years out in her estimation of his life span and what's more there was no way he could ever be described as an angel.

Dad's withered arm was due to complications with TB after he fell down a cellar grate when he was less than two years old. My recently rediscovered Great Aunt Gladys was able to give more details about the accident. Apparently my Grandma was walking to the shops with uncle Frank and nearly two year old baby Lewis (my dad) toddling on behind. Dad fell straight down an open cellar grate and, before Grandma could do anything about it, the coal man threw a bag of coal down on top of him.

Shepherd kids in Whitsuntide clothes visiting Aunty for a donation

I am sure that the complication of TB was the real problem with his arm. He was in and out of King Edward's Hospital throughout his young life. There must have been some sad cases in there but I don't think many spirits were broken. My dad and other kids were still mischievous enough to get sent to the "Round House" when they misbehaved. This was apparently the equivalent of the punishment block and my dad says he did his time in there on several occasions.

On his fourteenth birthday his name was mentioned on the BBC Light Programme because it was his first birthday spent out of hospital since he was one year old.

The most serious effect of all was on his education and though he could get the gist of newspaper reports and sign his name he was never known to write much.

Presumably he was naturally right handed and was forced by circumstances to be left handed. This would only exacerbate the effect of his poor literacy.

Consequently he passed on all domestic clerical duties to my mother. She looked after the bills and household transactions as well as managing a knife glazing machine, our household budget, three kids, my dad, a dog, various cats and anyone else in the neighbourhood who needed help.

Dad's knowledge of classical poetry was totally inconsistent with his status in life and I assume that it resulted from the intermittent education he received from peripatetic teachers who visited the long term hospital residents, doing their best to give them some sort of mental stimulation.

Dad couldn't work out the rent money but he knew plenty about the green eyed yellow idol to the north of Kathmandu - vital information for a cutlery worker from Sheffield 5.

The story goes that when my dad was a young man my grandma, conscious of his handicap, had skimped and saved to set him up in a little corner shop but he quickly gave up the idea, saying he was not a "non producer" and he wanted to do a proper man's job!

I have always assumed that part of this "producer" pride must have stemmed from war time propaganda intended to give status and pride to the factory workers who had not been called up to fight in the war.

Perhaps it was also tied in with the strong socialism and trade unionism of the day.

Like most Sheffielders at the time, dad always voted Labour but it didn't stop him criticising everything the council and the government did.

His favourite expression was "If Labour put up a spice pig with a currant eye round here it would get voted in." and some would say they did, and they were.

The day came when my dad had to go into Nether Edge hospital for quite a long time. His weight went down below nine stones and his breathing became poor. It turned out to be TB caused by the grinding dust from his job. He was in there for several months but later was allowed out sometimes for a few hours at a time.

He was doing occupational therapy whilst in hospital and one day brought home a magnificent half-moon shaped hearthrug with a jet black background which complemented the beautiful arrangement of brightly coloured posies of flowers arrayed in the centre. It was made of proper wool strands, not strips of old coats and blankets like the existing pegged rug on our hearth, which we had all helped to make.

My mam gazed at the new rug in awe for ages then declared "I don't think it would look right in our house, it's too nice - it would stick out like a sore thumb." Tact and diplomacy were conspicuous by their absence in our house and my dad never forgave her for this till the day he died but it has to be said, mam was right. It would have looked ridiculous on top of our ripped and worn congoleum. (Now there's a blast from the past. Congoleum was a cheap and nasty substitute for linoleum, made mostly from pitch and paper. But you knew that surely.)

As a result of Dad's TB the three of us kids had to go for regular health checks at Queens Road Clinic. I remember my brother once fainting at the TB clinic and all he was having was an X Ray.

A young nurse tried to catch him but he scratched himself on something and drew blood as he went down, which caused concern even in those pre-litigation days. As I recall, we were at the clinic without Mam or Dad being there, but this didn't seem at all strange to us. She had to go to work.

The good news was that after contact with the TB I had built up immunity and didn't go through the painful process which produced a nasty long lasting scab on the upper arm that the less fortunate had to allow to drop off before they could take part in rough and tumbles. The scab that is, not the arm.

When it came to dishing out the stuff from Harvest Festival and we were asked if we knew anyone old, poor or sick, I refrained from saying "Yes, all three!"

One particular playground game for the less gentle types was to go around thumping the TB jab victims hard on the upper arm as a kind of TB test of their own. Some of the perpetrators had the jabs themselves and even the most timid of victims would be so infuriated that they would do "same back". I don't know how many mis-diagnosed cases resulted when the doctors did their post-immunisation check to find hundreds of recovering TB scabs surrounded by extensive bruising. Still this was one playground war I was glad to be out of.

Any embarrassment associated with having TB in the family was minor compared with the day that teachers pulled me out of assembly having noticed I had impetigo. To their credit they were fairly discreet and I did get time off school, but I had to suffer alone at home all day and look after myself.

Another positive side to the TB business was that I became a free dinner. (I didn't EAT a free dinner, I BECAME a free dinner - that is the school terminology to this day according to our lass, who until recently was an infant teacher.) I don't remember any particular stigma attached to this despite the fact that we Free Dinners for some reason formed a separate queue with our non-dinner money on Monday mornings. Nowadays the free dinner transactions are carried out quite discreetly and rightly so.

When it came to dishing out the stuff from Harvest Festival and we were asked if we knew anyone old, poor or sick, I refrained from saying "Yes, all three!" but explained that my dad was in hospital with TB. Mr (personality) Wilson looked quite surprised.

As my class teacher it would have been nice if he had been already aware of any potentially sensitive issues in my life, but that outlook belongs to the modern day.

Nevertheless I was pleased to go home that day with a big bunch of flowers as well as a basket of fresh fruit and veg the likes of which we had not seen in the Shepherd house for a long time.

This was the only benefit of an otherwise meaningless Harvest Festival and to arrive at that point we had to endure the most boring sermon ever to be preached by a man of the cloth, namely Reverend Ball from St. Leonard's Church.

On one occasion he even had the audacity to title his sermon "Chewing on the Old Harvest Bone." The whole theme was based on the repetitiveness of his job. How inspiring. Needless to say half of us fell prostrate at his feet whilst the rest ran around shouting "I've seen the light!" No, not really. What we really did was yawn and mumble to each other, "What is this boring old fool on about?"

Anyway back to my dad. He was not embarrassed about his bad arm but had learned years ago that there was no advantage in advertising it and he always refused to have a Registered Disabled card. He once told me of an occasion when he got a job and did it well for six weeks until one day he got warm and rolled his sleeves up. The boss saw his arm and gave him his cards saying he was unsuitable for the job.

When Dad came out of Nether Edge hospital he was advised by the doctors not to go back into the dust of the grinding shop so when he went to the labour exchange they found him a job in the brickyard on Halifax Road, now appropriately called Kilner Way. He was operating a pan mill which crushed dry rock and clay down to powder. Half the powder went into the brick making process and the rest went into my dad. After two or three months of this he was soon back in the cutlery works but this time he was able to get a different job away from the dust. He came home covered in grease instead.

This job was at Westhall Richardson's and my mam worked there as well. During this period our house was alive with strange conversations about buffing, glazing, double heading, whittle tangs, spelter bolsters etc. Some of these expressions will soon never be heard again in Sheffield.

I have an interest in language and dialect, and one of my favourite words heard at home was daytal, meaning fixed wage as opposed to piecework. Daytal could also mean slow and stupid in our house but I have never heard the word spoken outside our family, nor have I seen it in any book on Yorkshire dialect.

See, I told you the dialect words were dying out.

Get Thi Neck Weshed

Having grown up in this atmosphere it is no surprise that to this day I am obsessed with my old pen knife collection which includes a couple made by my hero Stan Shaw, the last man on earth who can, and still does, produce proper pen knives by hand, doing every part of the process himself. I feel privileged to know this quietly spoken, unassuming man whose interest in the trade is as strong now as when he started as an apprentice over seventy years ago.

Like all true Dee Dahs, whenever I dine out, whilst waiting for the soup I use the time to look closely at the quality and origin of the cutlery. But nowadays if I stuck to my principles and refused to eat whenever the cutlery is not from Sheffield I would be a very hungry man indeed. (I still stick to these principles at home, having searched around various second hand stalls but it is getting more difficult and anyway the wife tries to dissolve the knife handles in the dishwasher. (What can you expect? She's from Liverpool.)

My mam, like dad and many other Sheffielders had suffered occupational health problems in the past. When she was a young girl she worked in a plating shop and had chromic acid dripping constantly from the work onto an inadequate leather apron, then down onto her leg, leading eventually to septicaemia.

After eleven weeks in hospital it looked as if she might lose her leg but the doctor decided to try a newly discovered treatment and she managed to recover, though she was left with a hole almost as big as an egg in her right leg. The system of compensation in those days was much more straightforward than it is today. You didn't get any.

I think mam and dad were popular at work and we had lots of visitors who would start the buffing / glazing / double heading / whittle tang conversation all over again.

One particular young woman called Eileen was what my mother described as loud, and flighty - not Mams' type at all.

Eileen appeared along with other whittle-tang spelter bolster makers, early on Christmas Eve and was given a welcoming drink of gin by my dad. I don't think it was the first gin of the day and it certainly wasn't the last. In fact it was helped along with that other Christmas delicacy, Egg Flip, whatever that might be.

Everyone at home was in bed but we managed to locate, and empty, the precious bottle of Christmas sherry without disturbing them.

Nobody on Parson's Cross really knew how much spirit constituted a proper tot, which explains how deadly quiet it was around the estate on Christmas mornings. (I have to confess that the strength of spirits still takes me by surprise, if waiting till next morning for the effects can be described as a surprise.)

Anyway, after a few more liberal applications of gin, Eileen treated us to her rendition of various popular drunken pub songs of the day, and the amazing thing is that she pre-empted the trade mark of that slightly more famous singer, Lulu, who at that point had never even set her child- size 3s on stage. Eileen started every song in Lulu style well before Lulu's time, with the now familiar

"We-ie-ie-eeeeil."

I would like to report that a good time was had by all, but my mother, who didn't drink much, was in charge of the tight budget and didn't like Eileen anyway, tried to break up the party by hiding the gin, whereas Dad, who was all for hospitality, Christmas spirit and to hell with tomorrow, was all for keeping the party going. I have to say I was with Dad on this occasion. Many years later I was guilty of repeating history by inviting a workmate home after early release on the last day of work. Everyone at home was in bed but we managed to locate, and empty, the precious bottle of Christmas sherry without disturbing them.

Next morning my mother got up and managed to go out to town to buy the last remnants of Christmas shopping from the market, whilst ignoring the complete stranger asleep on the settee. Her only comment was on the sideboard, written, as usual, on the triangular corner of an old envelope.

"Better get another bottle of Sherry!"

Another regular visitor to our humble abode was called Ronnie. In my very early childhood he used to turn up at our house regularly to swap his tea coupons for spice coupons. It seems unfair now that a family with three kids would part with their spice coupons in exchange for tea coupons but at the time tea was a necessity of life and spice were a luxury we could not afford. (Spice is the proper word for what non Sheffielders call sweets. I mention this in readiness for when my book hits the global market.)

Ronnie was about four foot six and extremely thin. His voice can only be described as soprano and not until I was middle aged did I realise that for some medical reason Ronnie had never reached puberty. Perhaps that's why he preferred sweets coupons to tea coupons.

Ronnie dedicated his life to charity and was well known throughout Sheffield for visiting pubs with various collecting tins. He was often portrayed in The Star for breaking some tin rattling record or other and despite his shortcomings (if you'll pardon the expression) he had a fulfilling life and a very wide circle of friends.

Another regular visitor, a war veteran called Ted, was a great romancer and told the most incredible stories which went on forever, all of which started with the same words for which he became famous..."When I was in Burma..." On hearing this everyone would either remember an urgent appointment or cringe and prepare themselves for a long trek through a jungle of lies and make believe.

Ted had three or four kids Once again our parents assumed that if Ted was their friend, then his kids would be our friends, so we went several times on our own on the bus to a crowded house full of strangers in Pitsmoor.

Ted's wife was Maltese and very friendly, but quite loud and excitable. His younger daughter Marguerite had Spina Bifida and never went outside but was a very exuberant child, who welcomed me with a loud "Hello Graham" before we had been introduced.

The older girl Andrea was my sister's age, dark complexioned and very beautiful. Norma and Andrea met up occasionally for a day out and inevitably I was dragged along. I enjoyed these trips out but with hindsight it was two teenagers on the loose with a burden of a kid brother tagging along.

Another workmate called Edgar was known at work to be quite a good singer and one day persuaded my mam and dad (and me) to go and hear him sing formally in his own environment.

It turned out to be something called a Four Square Mission meeting, full of people seeing the light, singing "Let the Fire Fall" and shouting out Hallelujah at random opportunities throughout the evening. The congregation got quite excited at our arrival, thinking that three more souls were about to be saved. Indeed Edgar's excellent singing voice was enough to convert the devil himself but not quite enough to convert the Shepherd family.

Another of my dad's friends from the cutlery works was a chap known affectionately as Sailor Bold. He and his wife and kids used to come to us on Saturdays or we would go to their house down Hillsborough. It was a small terraced house and they spent their entire life crammed into the kitchen. The front room was immaculately kept but was a no go area for family and visitors alike. It was only there for dusting.

The routine was for the adults to go for a pint in the Freemasons whilst I, at the tender age of ten or eleven, was considered old enough to take charge of their two younger lads on the strict understanding that we were not to go outside. I repaid their trust by waiting until they had gone round the corner before taking the kids out to wander the streets or play out on the Limbrick.

On more than one occasion we would go all the way to Rivelin Valley and play around the ponds catching tadpoles and frogs. I recall at that time there was still an old broken waterwheel next to a ruined mill building. How old am I for heaven's sake? Eventually Mam and Dad and Mr. and Mrs. Sailor Bold would come back to find us sitting innocently watching their telly with tousled hair, scabby knees and covered in muck and pond weed from head to foot.

One particular visitor from the factory stayed for a longer period; in fact his visit ran into years. He was a teenager, about five foot six, weighed about seven stone and I will call him Dave because that was not his name. He called in one day to say goodbye to my mam and dad as he was off to London.

He couldn't stay where he was any longer and had nothing else going for him around Sheffield so he came to say goodbye to the Shepherds. A wise decision, though a little transparent considering the large suitcase he had with him!

One of our house rules was that when the Big Ben chimes came on the radio the call would go out "Nine o'clock. Get to bed." My brother is six years older than me and my sister four years older, but the same rule applied to us all. Nine o'clock get to bed.

I often think how lucky I am to be blessed with a close family, none of whom would ever let another go in need of help. By comparison the only port Dave could turn to in the storm of his troubled life was the home of Lewis and Ada Shepherd. These casual friends and former workmates were the nearest he ever got to a stable family.

As time went by Dave settled in and I think our family appreciated his modest financial donation. He called my mam "Mam" and pretended to all his friends that I was his brother. I think he even called himself Shepherd whenever he could get away with it with strangers.

I never got to know much about his past life but occasionally there were little insights into how it must have been. He once saw an electric razor of my dad's and remarked with fond affection that he once had one exactly the same, which he had bought on HP.

When I asked where it was now he looked a bit downcast and just said "My mother sold it, but it's nearly paid for now." That one sentence revealed a whole sad story of a life in which family relationships, financial inadequacy and ethical behaviour were on a different plane to the relatively stable life I have been fortunate enough to live, despite my occasional whinge. Dave's life when he first came under the Shepherd wing could have gone in any direction except upward. But when I last heard of him he was working, happily married to a decent girl and had a grown up child.

One of our house rules was that when the Big Ben chimes came on the radio the call would go out "Nine o'clock. Get to bed." My brother is six years older than me and my sister four years older, but the same rule applied to us all. Nine o'clock get to bed.

The BBC watershed was pre-empted by fifty years. No wonder I was always knackered at school.

69

In winter the house was freezing away from the immediate vicinity of the fireplace. If we complained we were usually told not to be so nesh.

In winter the house was freezing away from the immediate vicinity of the fireplace. If we complained that the bed was cold we were usually told to not be so nesh, but on the coldest days we would take the oven shelves and oven door to bed wrapped in old cushion covers. We thought this was great fun.

Bed time story must be the most significant, cherished, intimate loving moments in the development of the human character. I will confirm this the first time anyone ever reads me one. I don't remember ever seeing a children's book in our house.

It seems to me that in those days rearing children meant keeping them fed and clothed, and trying, with limited success, to stop them from swearing or being cheeky. There was never much parental consideration for children's education, emotional well being or character development. An "upbringing" on Parson Cross and Shercliff was rare indeed. We just didn't have 'em.

To be fair I did know three school mates who had an upbringing. Each was an only child of a mum (Yes they had mums, not mams) who didn't work and one of them lived in a real private house. One became Head Boy, another went on to King Edward's School.

The third made an even greater social and educational advancement. He moved away!

Once in bed, me and our Alan would get into deep conversation. He would explain quite complex scientific matters which fascinated me but eventually, he being so much older and also very clever, would go far beyond my understanding. Nevertheless he was one of the few educational influences in my life and had more effect on my future than did the teachers at Shercliff School.

Often when we had been instructed to shut up and go to sleep we would get under the bed clothes and whisper down a secret length of hose pipe stretched out between the beds. Most of the basic principles of science which have entered my understanding and shaped the rest of my education and indeed my career have come to me via two yards of black rubber tube. Perhaps this method of communication should be tried in schools instead of computer whiteboards. It worked for me.

Our Norma was a bit more frivolous than Alan and used to make up games or invent stories and bring herself down to my level when we played together. One Christmas she got me to write a letter to Santa and we threw it into the chimney where it immediately flew up in the up-draught. A minute or two later a reply from Santa, addressed to me and referring to all my requests, came floating down.

To this day she still refuses to explain how she did the trick and insists it was a genuine reply from Santa. And she expects me to believe it. It has just occurred to me that may be if I refuse to supply any more Henderson's Relish she might be persuaded to divulge the secret. I have already missed the opportunity of playing the trick on my own kids. Perhaps Norma may relent in time for my grandchildren but I don't know where we will we find an open fireplace to perform the trick.

I do recall one episode where Norma's larking about went too far. It had just become fashionable for young teenage girls to put faint streaks in their hair as a small token of their individualism.

There was a level of peroxide application which parents and teachers would not even notice, whilst giggly friends in the corner of the school yard could be whipped up into a frenzy of admiration of one's daring rebelliousness. This was the level of peroxide which Norma accurately applied to her mousy locks.

Unfortunately she had a bit of peroxide left over!

Like a lamb to the slaughter I was drawn in to the naughty, adventurous, giddy game that was Norma. With words like "let's just try it" and "I won't do it too much" and "it's not very strong" and "nobody will notice" I was coaxed to sit down and succumb to her frivolous plan. Unfortunately it is a scientific fact that wet hair looks darker, whilst peroxided wet hair looks normal brown until it is dry.

All this occurred when I was about thirteen and going through all the normal teenage angst about how I looked, how others thought of me, what status I was maintaining in the hierarchy and worst of all, what the girls would make of the only streaky haired schoolboy in Sheffield.

At least one girl, who previously shared shy, interested, knowing looks with me, reverted to giggling to her stupid mates whenever I approached. One thing was certain. At that time, dyeing your hair was a girl thing. It was not for hard, show-off men who fancied themselves, it was not for beatniks or teddy boys, it was not for pop stars and it was not even for gays, because gays had not been invented then. And it was certainly, explicitly, definitely not for Parson Cross lads. No. It was just girls, and me! My life was ruined.

Norma, I love you, but next time I see you I will smack you round the head. At one time Alan and Norma would speak to each other in a secret language called the Agy Pagy language and I had no idea what they were saying. But they could never be horrible to me for long and soon explained the secret code. All they were doing was saying "age" between each syllable, so a phrase like "Where are you going" would become "Whage-ere age-are yage-ou g-age-o-age-ing" etc. If you speak quickly like this it is difficult for those not in the know, to follow the conversation. (It is safe to try this at home folks, but don't say it was me who told you, because I was sworn to secrecy back in 1953)

I don't know what would have become of me without the influence of my brother and sister, who both seemed to enjoy my company despite the fact that on many occasions looking after me must have been more of a duty than an option for them. Thinking back on all this, I am quite envious that I didn't have a younger sibling, though I never thought about this at the time.

On at least one occasion Norma even went up see my teachers on open night because my mam and dad were completely out of their natural environment in the presence of the educated classes such as teachers. Having Alan to elevate me to his scientific level, entertaining me with factual stories, and Norma having fun with me at my own level, I would like to think that their different approaches complemented each other and had a lasting positive effect on my character as well as contributing to my day to day happiness in a childhood which otherwise did not have a lot going for it.

Usually our parents weren't in during school holidays or when we got home from school and I was the proverbial latch key kid.

My first and most hated job was lighting the fire. When it wouldn't go it had to be drawn up with a sheet of newspaper which made it roar like mad. Often the paper would suck in and catch fire. Option one was to quickly screw the burning paper up and throw it onto the freezing flameless coal but if it all happened too fast the blazing paper would fly up the chimney, in grave danger of setting the chimney on fire. At ten to nine in a morning, from Shercliff school yard one could look back at a few hundred chimneys and it was not unusual to see one with massive plumes of black smoke and soot billowing forth, soon followed by the clang of the fire engine.

Alternatively the amusing sight of a chimney sweep's brush would sometimes suddenly appear cartoon fashion from one of the chimneys and do a little twizzle before disappearing back down again.

If ever any of us unexpectedly left the house empty we had an established procedure.

Everyone will tell you that in the old days nobody bothered to lock their doors. This is a myth on a par with the sun shining all summer, snow falling all winter and school days being the happiest days of your life. Anyway we were not so trustworthy at our house. We would lock the door and put the key under the door mat. Just to avoid any confusion a note would be written, on the inevitable triangular flap from a used envelope. The note was pinned to the door immediately above the mat, which in any case was so thin, and the key so thick that not only could it be seen, one could almost copy the shape without even shifting the mat. The note read:-

"KEY UNDER MAT"

Maybe most of the people in Sheffield 5 were honest (which I believe was the case.) Maybe if there were any would-be burglars in the area they could not read. Maybe a procession of thieves went in every day, found nothing worth pinching, locked up after themselves and replaced the key under the mat. In any event we were never burgled.

To me this little story sums it all up. The naivety, the chaos of our lives, the absence of logic and the trust in human nature.

It was all portrayed in three words on the back of an old envelope. And if the system failed, which it didn't very often, we only needed to ask the

Our Alan tells of earlier days when my mam would hold me in one arm whilst preparing food at the same time.

neighbours because all the keys on the estate fitted another back door somewhere along the street. And the last resort of all was for me to climb through the tiny pantry window, which a scrawny little brat like me could manage with ease.

Meals at our house were always haphazard affairs. For a start our corn flakes and milk were always served on a flat dining plate because the only bowls we had were glass ones kept for tinned fruit when Auntie Rosie came to tea every sixth Sunday.

I must have been quite shy when I was small because one day when a load of relatives from Ecclesfield turned up I went into my "Den" behind the settee.

It was decided that fish and chips were required and the room was alive with "I want a fish cake" "I'll have a fish and share your chips" and so on. I waited to be asked but nobody crawled behind the settee to ask me. When the chips were distributed I emerged and gave a little cough to make my presence felt but still nobody noticed I was the only one not eating. I went up to my little cousin and said,

"Are they nice?"

My mother and one or two aunties suddenly realised and the air was filled with cries of "Ah! We've forgotten him, Ah! poor little luv." etc. (I am tempted here to say for comic effect that they still didn't give me any chips, but they did really.)

Our Alan tells of earlier days when my mam would hold me in one arm whilst preparing food at the same time. When this involved cutting bread my little head would rock amusingly from side to side as she held me and the bread towards her with one arm and sawed away with the other. From a distance this must have looked like a scene from a horror film.

I survived intact but the slices of bread at our house always looked mutilated. The bread was sometimes spread with margarine but in those days this was frowned on even by the humblest people.

We always had a "Butter Cooler" which contained "Bess Butter."

Mam's method of application was to use the bread knife to spread a luscious thick layer onto the end of the loaf until our little mouths drooled, then scrape it all off again until hardly any remained. The surplus, by now fifty per cent crumbs, was then scraped back into the "butter cooler." (Why on earth was it called butter cooler?)

So how would I summarise the quality of life in my childhood compared with today? Well nowadays my neck never gets noticeably mucky and I haven't cut my knee for ages. Neither do I get chilblains, grit in my eye or boils or verrucas. Nobody legs me up or gives me a dead leg and I haven't had the cane for a long time.

I have many fond memories as this book will testify but there were aspects of life which, with the disadvantage of hindsight, did not seem so sweet. I must have been in cynical mood when I tried to sum up the situation in the following poem.

The Best Years of Your Life??

When cabbage was compulsory
and black and sour and sad
Where they paid no heed though
I would plead that the turnip had
gone bad
Where THEY dictated what I ate
despite my trembling voice
Condemned me to THEIR recipes,
the menu of no choice

Where the food, (I loosely use the
word) came in a dull grey tray
In a dull grey van I used to hope
would crash along the way
But the gristly stew, the lumpy
mash, the gravy's limpid pool
Had advantage o'er this retching
wretch - it was from another school!

Where curtains, rotting from effects
of greeny yellow fog
Were opened slight to watch a fight
about a neighbour's dog
Where frying pans and pokers were
waved in anger too
Their mood was black, their eyes
burned red, their language royal blue
(And that was just the women!)

When dark and itchy trousers run up
on mam's machine
Caused me such embarrassment so
shameful to be seen
For even at that tender age I was
wise enough to note
The tweedy brown resemblance to
my mam's discarded coat

75

Get Thi Neck Weshed

When boots were black and hankies
grey there was a rosy glow
To noses, shining cherry red, with
greenish stripes below
On winter's nights, no light to see
Mother Nature's cruel trick
Black ice inside the toilet a good two
inches thick
And not until hot water was
obtained the following day
Were the little squares of Sheffield
Star - Et Cetera - flushed away

When washday came on winter's
morn, no comfort to be had
No access to the pantry and my
mother hopping mad

With dripping on the table and
dripping sheets above
Carbolic in the atmosphere, no time
for mother love
In the freezing room the failing fire
could only just be seen
Through holes in winter woollies all
hanging round the screen

So please let's not romanticise those
glorious days gone by
Were childhood days such happy
days? Let me expose the lie
Let's not forget the misery, the
tedium and strife
Appreciate adulthood, the best
years of your life.

On rare occasions my mam would take me with her to town. I remember once when very small, losing her in Tupholmes in Pitsmoor. I ran around crying, reaching up to every fat woman in a tweedy coat which roughly matched my home made trousers, but they all said "I'm not your mummy" until I eventually found the right one. This incident seemed to go on for hours but for all I know it might have been a few seconds.

On one occasion at Tupholmes I saw a television set. Yes. Honestly, a real television set, turned on and working! It was many years later before we got our own television, bought for four guineas from someone in the Magnet. The visit to Tupholmes proved to be a day of memorable experiences because as well as the television, I saw my first black man. We got on a bus which was full and my mam got the last seat, with me stood up beside her.

Across the aisle sat a middle aged black man, quite fat and extremely well dressed in a smart flashy suit, trilby hat and a very loud tie. He grabbed hold of me, sat me on his knee and when he smiled he showed

When he smiled he showed a mass of big teeth which were pure white except for one, which was solid gold. I had never seen anything like it and I regret I was a bit too shy to respond well to his open friendliness.

a mass of big teeth which were pure white except for one, which was solid gold. I had never seen anything like it and I regret I was a bit too shy to respond well to his open friendliness. After that we got used to seeing from the Shercliff bus, an increasing number of black people and one by one the shabby houses of Pitsmoor and Burngreave were gradually painted up in bright colours which we moderate British would have described as gaudy.

I don't recall any animosity towards black people in those days (We didn't call them black but went all around the houses to find supposedly polite alternative words) but rather than treating them as equals, society subjected them to a double dose of patronisation.

As an example, I recall what a pleasant novelty it was to board a bus on which the conductor was black, but one day a black man was actually driving the bus I was on. All little lads in those days dreamed of becoming a bus driver and the respect we youngsters had for bus drivers was equalled only by Flash Gordon and western film heroes. My young mind felt strangely uneasy about a black man in this exalted role. Where had I picked up this prejudice?

How had such a young, supposedly uncontaminated mind come up with a feeling of unease about such an inconsequential situation? As an adult all I can do is express shame and regret, and take comfort from the fact that I have, hopefully, risen above such an attitude.

We were all taught to love the British Empire and the House system at the Senior School divided us into supporters of Canada, New Zealand, Australia and South Africa, all countries into which, 'wider still and wider shall our bounds be set' as the song goes. At Junior School the houses were Nelson, Grenfell, Kingsley and Scott. One day I will read up who these people were and what they did, because nobody at school ever bothered to tell us.

Until then it had never occurred to me that any adult could be questioned let alone the British Government, but it is a lesson I have never forgotten.

Perhaps they did but I might have been larking about and not listening. Racial prejudice at the time was not helped by the constant news reports of the so called "Mau Mau Terrorists" who were rebelling in central Kenya. One day my mam after hearing yet another bad news report made a remark about the "terrorists" and our Alan replied, "Well, what would we British do if some foreigner came here and threw us off the land and stole our farms?" When put like that, my mam was immediately convinced and so was I.

I don't know where Alan got all this from at such an early age but it was certainly not in keeping with the national propaganda of the day. Until then it had never occurred to me that any adult could be questioned let alone the British Government, but it is a lesson I have never forgotten. A basic sense of right and wrong is as valid as government policy any day. It is called fairation.

Once again my brother and sister played a part in developing my attitudes when as teenagers they became active in multi national organisations and introduced into our family some friends from other nations. One such was Tony (Tai) from Zanzibar. My dad managed to get him a job in the cutlery works. His mate Hafith worked at Cann's music shop on Dixon Lane, repairing speakers and record players. The technology of the day was not difficult but Hafith managed to acquire the nick name of Hi-Fi. Other friends of theirs were Hungarian refugee students who had been involved in the 1956 revolution and had to escape the country in fear of their lives.

To their credit my mam and dad, who had little understanding of the wider world, took all Alan and Norma's foreign friends at face value and made them welcome in our home. Some of them thought the world of my mam and visited our house long after Alan and Norma had gone to university and moved on in life.

Alan and Norma once had a big party at our house and a Dansette record player supplied by Hi-Fi was left behind for ages along with several

What a grand piece of technology that was. It was second hand, presumably from the Magnet, and to call it portable was an infringement of the Trades Descriptions act

vinyl records, or were they bakelite at that time? (Incidentally Hi-Fi's party trick was to eat unwanted records. I can't remember if he spat the bits out or swallowed them but he certainly chewed them up into pieces.)

I used to come home alone from school at lunch time and play records like "I Don't Care if the Sun Don't Shine" at 78, 45, 33 and 16 rpm. If ever I hear that song at the correct speed today it sounds really strange.

Thus my musical interest was aroused and when Christmas came I tormented my dad into getting me a portable radio. What a grand piece of technology that was. It was second hand, presumably from the Magnet, and to call it portable was an infringement of the Trades Descriptions act. It was not a transistor set but was full of valves and was powered by two batteries. One was as big as a jam jar and the other was 90 volts and about the size and weight of a bag of sugar.

Anyone foolish enough to touch both terminals at once received quite a severe shock. The radio looked like a suit case and had one redeeming feature. It switched off by closing the lid, so it was possible for me to listen to Radio Luxemburg in bed by holding the lid up with one hand until, when I fell to sleep, my first restless movement would allow the lid to close thus preserving the batteries for another night of Top Twenty (sheet music) and adverts about BMK carpets.

If you asked my mother she would claim that she didn't "neighbour", the word neighbour being a verb in this context. She condemned others for gossipin'/callin'/cantin'/gassin' - a waste of valuable time which should be spent on domestic duties. (Men didn't need to be chauvinist in those days - the women did it for them). However this did not preclude her from the established practice of creating an excuse for social contact by lending, borrowing, sharing, giving and fetching things from town for neighbours. This kind of mutual help totally justified her interaction with those around her. And everything which was given, passed on, brought for or lent was ritually placed in a white paper bag so that others couldn't see what was

At that point the argument would cease immediately. The victor was the first one to utter the word "offended" having allowed the argument to go on for the traditionally acceptable length of time.

going on. In those days every paper bag, sheet of tissue paper, brown paper carrier, elastic band or piece of string (also called band) was kept in the top left hand sideboard drawer for re-use to keep prying eyes from the detail of the transaction.

This recycling process was a custom of the nineteen fifties culture which will be reinvented in the coming years as the necessity for recycling becomes accepted. When something of significant value was given to a neighbour the following protracted ceremonial conversation would ensue.

"Can I give you summat for it?"

"No, don't be silly"

"Go on, take this"

"No I don't want anything"

"Go on let me pay you for it"

"No, you can have it, honest"

"No, I'll feel awful, here take this"

"I've said no! Now put it away"

"Please, go on, let me..."

This well practiced ritual would go on indefinitely until one of the combatants chose the appropriate moment to deliver the coup de gras.

"If you don't take it I shall be offended!"

At that point the argument would cease immediately. The victor was the first one to utter the word "offended" having allowed the argument to go on for the traditionally acceptable length of time. The discussion would then taper off with just a few more comments, said at a gradually reducing volume.

"Well I don't want to take it really"

"It's all right. I want you to have it"

"I feel awful now"

It was a game requiring tremendous social skill and experience but all the women in Sheffield 5 were expert players.

Chapter Six
Mis-shaped Allsorts from Bassetts

One of the best gifts often given by neighbours was mis-shaped Allsorts from Bassetts. Half the women on the estate worked at Bassetts and could be seen every morning leaving the estate in droves, wearing their identical white turbans.

Our Norma once worked there for a summer job. One story she told was that one day she was introduced to an ancient lady who had been working a machine for nearly fifty years. Norma said something like "Oh. That's interesting, printing the word "Bassetts" on all those big sheets of liquorice." The lady replied "Oh. Is that what it is love? I've never really looked closely at it before."

Liquorice Allsorts on our estate were never of a regular shape. They were always bent, rounded where they should be square or with an extra layer in the sandwich, or no middle layer at all.

Occasionally there would be a big six inch lump which had not been cut up into separate pieces and all these misfits would be sold off to the factory workers and find their way onto the Parson Cross Estate. They would be passed around and would always be subject to the "Let me pay you" "No you can have it" routine.

Just one product was an exception to the "Go on, take it" rule. If the object in question happened to be a knife which had, perhaps, been "got from work" then a token payment, usually one penny, was expected. A knife could not be given. It had to be bought or the friendship would be severed for ever.

Any recipient who did not offer the penny would be reminded immediately, without any embarrassment and would promptly pay up. I love these old Sheffield traditions and would love to know how and when this one began.

Another regular procedure between neighbours, which seems quaint today, was the habit of sharing out hot water. If any was going spare on washday or after a big cleaning job one of us kids would be sent to ask

There was no "I'll tell your dad" at the Dobbos' house. He was as scared of her as the kids were, and everyone else on the estate for that matter.

neighbours if they wanted a bowl of the precious stuff, because it would be a shame to waste it. Housewives who had perhaps planned quite a different day for themselves would reconsider rather than waste a chipped enamel bowl full of Mrs. Shepherd's hot water and they would end up washing the best tea service or scrubbing the step.

May I just ask in passing, when did you last scrub your step? Is it any wonder that the world is full of disease when people leave their steps unscrubbed for two or three days at a time?

If I were to write about my last fifteen years instead of my first, neighbours would probably not even get a mention. But in those days neighbours were an integral part of our lives. Indeed some families around us could provide enough material for a book of their own, if not a library! Take for example the Dobbos.

Mrs. Dobbo had a husband as meek and mild as they come, and five kids who along with all residents of the estate, were terrified of her. She looked like a witch, thin as a rail with hatchet features, a sharp nose and a harsh shrieking voice. I would describe her eyes but nobody was ever known to make eye contact. To complete the terrifying image she had a vocabulary which would curdle milk. She once had a back yard fight with her next door neighbour, which went on for ten minutes and involved much blood, snot and black eyes.

Her language was, to use the uniquely Sheffield expression, outdacious. Her favourite term of endearment, frequently directed at her own children, would often echo across the back gardens,

"I'll kill thee tha bleedin' cow!"

There was no "I'll tell your dad" at the Dobbos' house. He was as scared of her as the kids were, and everyone else on the estate for that matter. When her youngest, Keefie, was born she bought a magnificent high slung pram on the never-never, which she had no hope of paying for. Rather than have it re-possessed she never used it but hid it behind the garden shed where it gradually filled up with water and rusted away. Poor little Keefie learned to walk at a very early age.

Mrs. Dobbo was always borrowing but since everyone avoided her, she usually sent the kids to do the errand.

She would not bother to tell them which house to go to, they just went from door to door saying something like "Me mam says have you got any brown sauce."

On one occasion the little girl went to the woman next door and said "Me mam says can she lend a bit of margarine and sugar and have you got a bit of flour?" The humour of the situation overcame the fear of Mrs. Dobbo and the lady replied

"Just tell her to send the bowl round and I will bake the cake for her."

The eldest girl Maureen managed to get a job as a domestic help working for a very rich family who owned a large furniture shop in town. Everyone on the street was enthralled to hear her little stories of life in a very unfamiliar level of society.

One of the biggest adjustments she had to make was that this respectable Jewish family were in the habit of giving guidance to their little boy with kind encouragement instead of a bunch of knuckles around the head.

Apparently there were many times when Maureen would scream "You little ......" and raise her fist above the infant head, only to change the blow to a fond stroke of the hair and her curse to "You little love" when she heard footsteps approaching.

The teenage Dobbo boy Tel was downright dangerous even when he was not on his racing Royal Enfield which he spent hours tuning every night before roaring off up the road in his shirt sleeves with no helmet on. His accomplice Kenny was easily led as he did not have a lot upstairs.

You will be familiar with the expression. 'The lights are on but there's nobody home.' Well in Kenny's case the lights weren't even on and the blinds were drawn.

Just by way of example, he once confided to me that he thought he had some kind of divine significance because as he walked the streets of Sheffield 5 at night the moon followed him around. All I can say is the moon made a strange choice.

Once she got going she made the Laughing Sailor machine at Cleethorpes sound like a manic depressive.

One day Tel and Kenny coaxed me into the house by telling me they had caught a big fish, which they offered to show me. They took me out of the front door and round the back but then declared the fish missing. They directed me back in through the back door which was ajar and when I pushed the door a very heavy electric iron fell just missing my head and making a hole in the lino. Attempted manslaughter was just their idea of amusement.

On another occasion Kenny shouted me in urgently saying Terry had been stabbed. When we went in he was staggering about dramatically then he fell down clutching in one hand a handkerchief covered in fake blood. In his other hand was a massive bowie knife which was certainly not a fake. When the joke was over he stood up, gave a blood curdling yell and threw the knife, splintering the door frame a few inches from me. How he got through life without killing someone I will never know. Perhaps he didn't.

Next door to us was an old couple who I will call Coultas because that was not their name. Owd Coultas was a jolly, rounded bloke, always with a trick up his sleeve, such as a Woopee cushion on the stool or a pile of imitation dog muck under it. One needed to be a little innocent infant to fall for the tricks. Perhaps that is why he liked my company.

I think Owd Lass Coultas was epileptic and before the Five Arches pub was built they always went for a drink in the Bull and Mouth on Castle Gate so as to be near the Shercliff bus stop in case of emergencies.

After eight at night anyone waiting at the row of corrugated iron bus stops would be treated to shrieks of fiendish laughter from Owd Lass Coultas in the Bull and Mouth dram shop.

Once she got going she made the Laughing Sailor machine at Cleethorpes sound like a manic depressive.

In years gone by Owd Man Coultas was one of Sheffield's last "Middin Men" but when the last flush toilet was installed in Sheffield he progressed to working at the Sheffield Incinerator where the contents of

the dustbins went. He was a good friend of mine and sometimes took
me with him when he went to work to collect his pay. For some strange
reason he, along with all other "Corporation" workers, was off work ill
for precisely thirteen weeks every year. Perhaps it was a mysterious
occupational malaise but I don't remember him ever displaying any
symptoms. Anyway during these times he still had to turn up once a week
for his wages. What a drudge.

If anything of the slightest value came in for incineration Owd Coultas,
having an early regard for global warming issues, would bring it home for
recycling and the Shepherd family were most conscientious in supporting
his green principles. (I'm glad we knew him after he had progressed from
the Middin job.) The incinerator, the whole process and the resulting
spoils were affectionately known as "Binzez."

The occasional toy or interesting utensil was most welcome but there
were other items, for which recycling was less appropriate. (Squeamish
readers might choose to omit a line or two here, though no refunds will be
payable.)

Some of the Binzez came from commercial premises. For example on
one occasion a pack of condensed milk jars (was it called connie onnie
or something?) was retrieved from a bin and distributed around for us to
savour. We lived on it for weeks.

Another time, a whole pack of chocolate bars was passed over the
Shepherd/Coultas fence. When opened it was found to be damp, mouldy
and green at one end but the other end looked normal. We made an
arbitrary decision on where to draw the line, literally, and shared out the
bits that looked most like chocolate - a rare treat for us kids who never saw
chocolate from one Christmas stocking to the next. As I have said before,
I hate it when old fogies say "Well, it didn't do me any harm!" but it has
to be acknowledged that here I am, alive and writing this book. All this
occurred before the days of sell by dates, a modern development which my
very survival has taught me to treat with a great deal of scepticism.

Neither Owd Coultas nor Owd Lass Coultas held any qualifications in
hygiene. One day I was going down our path when Owd Lass Coultas was
going up her path to the dustbin. In her hand was a plate containing a big
fat pork chop.

Get Thi Neck Weshed

On the chop was a layer of maggots writhing, jiggling and dancing about as if all their birthdays had come at once. She lifted the bin lid and when I expected to see her throw the meat in, she proceeded to hold the chop down with her dirty thumb and flick the maggots off into the bin. I'll swear they were breeding faster than she could flick. Despite my tender years I managed to persuade her to flick a bit harder and throw the lot away or someone would die.

On reflection I assume that she would not have paid for the meat anyway as she had a reputation for shoplifting and begging from stallholders in the Market Hall.

Owd Coultas had an interest in football and was a Wednesdayite. I had often observed the carnival atmosphere as loads of Wednesday supporters walked down Herries Road past our house.

Tipper lorries with twenty or so men standing in the back would pass by and I imagined them all being tipped out onto the ground outside the Spion Kop.

As the droves returned me and my mate would stand at our gate and cheekily ask passers by one after the other, "How've they gone on?" We need not have asked as the smiles or frowns said it all and anyway we had already counted the cheers and groans echoing up Herries road. Often we were ignored especially if Wednesday had lost, and quite often someone would give a result different from the general consensus. Either they were pulling our legs in retaliation or, like me, they didn't understand football.

Occasionally Owd Coultas would take me to the football match. The excitement of my first visit was heightened as my mother made an attempt to clean my face with spit on her hanky and rub my shoes, with the same hanky, so as not to "Show Owd Coultas up" though I protested quite rightly, with the immortal words for which I, and he, became famous "He dun't care Owd Coultas!"

Everyone burst into laughter at such a philosophical observation from such young lips, and it became a sort of catch phrase in the Shepherd household for years to come.

My own view was that like all catch phrases there was nothing funny about it whatsoever.

Get Thi Neck Weshed

Me and Owd Coultas would walk off down Herries Road and I would be lifted over the old steel turnstile, presumably because I was too young to pay, or at least so we claimed.

In truth I was not over interested in football except that I collected football cards, given out with sweet cigarettes I think. (I wonder why Nat Lofthouse cards were so rare when he was such a good player?) I remember almost freezing to death on one occasion and crying my eyes out but Old Coultas seemed unaware of my plight. Once during a match I tried to muster up some interest and asked Owd Coultas which one was Derek Dooley.

I had heard the song about "Dooley the Red Haired Giant" (to the tune of Rudolf the Red Nosed Reindeer) and couldn't see any red haired giants on the pitch. "Nay lad," Old Coultas replied, "I can't afford to watch him, these wot we come to see are just the reserves."

The football trips came to a sudden end when one day owd Coultas was knocked down by a motor bike on the Zebra crossing outside our house. The bike, rider and Owd Coultas ended up a tremendous distance from the crossing and Owd Coultas lay screaming with pain, his pelvis badly smashed.

All this was a most horrific sight for a young lad to witness and I remember it as though it was yesterday. It was many months before he gained any sort of mobility and for the rest of his days he used to walk around using a quaint old home made walking stick which is now one of my treasured possessions.

Owd Lass Coultas had a nickname which I was instructed never to repeat as it was greatly embarrassing and upsetting to her. The legend of "Traykle Annie" according to my dad stems from long before my time, when treacle was such a popular commodity that it was carted around in big barrels on a horse and cart.

One day a barrel fell from a cart and burst open on the road. Rather than waste the treacle a few local citizens came out with bowls and spoons to take a free sample.

Owd Lass Coultas was shameless, excitable, greedy and clumsy – a fateful combination under the circumstances. She ran up with a massive bowl and ladle, elbowed everyone out of the way and pushed to the front.

In the early years the Coultasses had a lodger. That is until I reduced their income somewhat by killing him.

Reaching over into the centre of the heap she lost her balance and fell headlong. As she struggled to get up, her hands slid forward and her feet slipped back until she was flat out, covered all down her front and stuck to the floor. The gathering crowd were helpless with laughter and nobody wanted to touch or assist her, so realising a different approach was necessary she decided to roll herself out. When Owd Coultas was finally fetched out to rescue her, her hair, clothes and undergarments were completely treacled back and front. Traykle Annie certainly succeeded in going home with a bigger share of treacle than everyone else though none of it was in her bowl.

In the early years the Coultasses had a lodger. That is until I reduced their income somewhat by killing him. It happened like this.

Owd Burton was very old and not very well. One day my Mam gave me a small, ribbed green bottle and told me to take it next door to Owd Burton who already knew what it was and was expecting it. I knocked on the door and called out "'s only me". Nobody answered so I entered and went upstairs where he was just getting out of his sick bed wearing the fashionable night attire of the time, which comprised of exactly the same as day attire except for the absence of trousers.

"What's this?" he grunted as I held out the bottle.

"My Mam's sent it" I replied.

"She says you know about it."

He put the bottle to his lips and took a couple of good hard swigs. His face screwed up a little displaying no sign of satisfaction or recognition and what's more there was no instant miracle cure for all his ills.

I went home and my Mam asked me if I had given him the bottle. "Yes, I gave it him and he had a drink." I replied.

Mam's face went ghastly white and she grabbed on to the kitchen sink for support.

With a look of horror she made me repeat it twice before she rushed next door in a panic. When she called upstairs and asked Owd Burton if he had drunk the liquid he said,

"Nay lass, I only smelt at it." So she left it at that.

The next thing to happen to Owd Burton was that he was dead. Hopefully a long time elapsed between the bottle episode and his death, and perhaps the two events were unrelated but I have told the story just as I remember it and I have been concerned about it ever since, though I never found out what was in the bottle. I am sure it will be too late now to have his body exhumed. Owd Burton was in quite an advanced state of decay even when he was alive.

The next people to join the Coultas family were the Wrights, a young couple with a little girl. They were extremely nice and respectable but I don't know how they came to be so desperate that the Coultas household was the best situation they could secure for themselves.

Mrs. Wright often escaped over to our house in tears and poured her heart out to my mother but I was too young to know what it was about. Little Marilyn was a cute two year old and was often left with us for a few hours as respite from the squalor of her life next door.

Once she was playing under our table when she did a wee on a pair of my socks, a crime for which I was able to admonish her mercilessly some twenty years later when I danced with her at midnight on New Year's Eve at the City Hall. For some strange reason she wouldn't date me after that. I was a teenager when Owd Coultas got cancer. His bed was brought down stairs and he lived out his life within a few feet of the bed and the old commode placed beside it.

I sometimes assisted him with his bodily functions in the undignified last days of his humble life. It was not the image a young man wished to cultivate for himself and my mother went spare about it but it was the least I could do for an old friend.

When Owd Lass Coultas passed away shortly after him, our family assisted with the clearance of the house. In a cupboard I found a live shell about eighteen inches long. If it came from Binzez then the Waste Operatives at Bernard Road incinerator owe their lives to the fact that he intercepted it before it went into the furnace.

After a long hard life which they enjoyed to the full, the total assets of the Coultas family including the house clearance amounted to four pounds ten shillings.

Get Thi Neck Weshed

The next tenant in the Coultas house was Derek Gadeed. As a Somalian he was a bit of a pioneer, the first black person ever to appear on the council estate. I don't know if the council applied any diplomacy but his situation was certainly eased by placing him between the Shepherds and kind hearted old Mrs. Hawksworth on the other side. Derek himself was a bit of a celebrity amongst the Somalis in Sheffield, working as a sort community representative. He once got invited to a Town Hall reception and decked himself out in a black suit, white shirt and a bowler hat - a rare sight indeed at the Shercliff bus stop.

I liked Derek and used to chat to him, learning a little bit about the Muslim culture.

One day he announced that his wife was coming from Somalia and he showed us a picture of a beautiful girl about twenty years his junior. On reflection I don't think he had met her at that point but she came over and settled down with him, eventually having two little girls. The poor woman couldn't speak a word of English and must have felt a bit isolated but once again my mam was able to make a difference and she and her two babies were often made welcome in our house. Unfortunately, for reasons unknown the marriage didn't last and they eventually went away to a refuge in Sheffield, leaving Derek on his own in the house. Right up to her death my mam, having moved away from the area, received the occasional card saying "Happy Eid" and such like.

Next door the other way was a very old couple who had a son Harry who was about the same age as my dad. One Saturday Harry called in the Bull and Mouth and met up with Owd Coultas who was blind drunk. My dad came home on the same bus with them, and he and Harry had to hold Owd Coultas up and steer him down Teynham Road. Harry's old mum looked out of her window and saw a trio of figures zig-zagging down Teynham Road and did her nut, shouting and bawling and refusing to let Harry in the house. The poor bloke had only drunk one pint until his bus came and my dad hadn't even been in the pub.

Another bloke called Eugine lived with them in the early days and he became a bit of a friend of mine, though we couldn't understand each other's conversation.

I think he might have been Polish or German or something.

Further down the road lived a rather unnerving character known as Loopy Luke. He was in his forties, a bachelor and strange as they come. He didn't mix well and obviously had his own problems.

It seems to me that the posh modern council houses were too big for their tenants who had moved in from "down't owd way" and nobody liked to see facilities wasted. Unofficial lodgers were a common way of subsidising the rent.

Further down the road lived a rather unnerving character known as Loopy Luke. He was in his forties, a bachelor and strange as they come. He didn't mix well and obviously had his own problems. He lived with his frail old mother and it was obvious that they were slowly driving each other barmy. One day there was a big disturbance at their house with much shouting and raving. Loopy Luke asked if he could bring his mam into our house until they all calmed down. (Why was it always the Shepherd's house?) They came in and the shouting started again intermittently but gradually quietened down. The old lady said he had been hurting her but all the bruises were on her wrists and consistent with his story that he had been restraining her when she got agitated.

After much counselling and cups of tea normal service was resumed and they went home peacefully.

On a later occasion Loopy Luke lost it completely and was last seen walking into the back of a Black Maria with a policeman on each arm, shouting "Look at me everybody, I'm barmy!" (Luke, not the policemen.) I would say his assessment was fairly accurate.

Another family of our acquaintance were the Bighams, they of the abandoned rabbit in the Morgan road gutter years earlier. Like us they moved from Morgan Road and lived three houses up from us. When we mused on how Mr. and Mrs. Bigham slept in a three bedroomed house with nine kids, my dad used to say that they sent the kids to bed in turn and when each one was asleep he was stood up in the corner and the bed handed over to the next in line.

There was a time when I believed all this.

Get Thi Neck Weshed

The youngest boy Lol was often in our house though I have no idea why and I have never even questioned it until now. My mam liked to ask him what he had had for tea. He always said the same thing, "Bwa" (meaning bread) to my mam's great amusement.

On a good day he would mumble that there was margarine or jam on it, but this was obvious as the evidence was spread around his face and down his jumper, covering dried remains from the day before. Incidentally, margarine in those days was frowned upon, as was brown bread. It took half a century for the experts to convince us otherwise and now both are back in fashion.

Mr. Bigham was not too good at writing but when he got a tax form, rent demand or a red electric bill he would write "NINE KIDS" straight across it and send it back. This simple statement was worth a thousand words and the recipients got the message loud and clear. You can't get blood out of a stone.

When we had an item of clothing or pair of shoes no longer fit for use - and some of our own stuff was already second hand - we would pass them on to the Bighams. They had a child to fit every size and type of attire anyone could come up with. Despite this, judging by their appearance I am sure they must have got up every morning and put each other's clothes on. They were a very ragged bunch with not a lot upstairs but nevertheless they were all quiet, well behaved, pleasant and polite.

Our Alan was in the Scouts and one day persuaded me to try the Cubs. I borrowed a cap and neckerchief and toddled off to St. Leonard's Church. I didn't know anyone and nobody knew me, introduced me or welcomed me. The cubs were all sitting round in a circle discussing the final details of an imminent camping trip which was not relevant to me. Afterwards there was a game which involved standing in a line and doing movements at the proper time. I only had a vague idea what was going on and ended up with knobbly legs apart in a long line of cubs with knobbly legs together, much to the disgust of the Akela.

I have often reflected, if that evening had been managed differently I would have got involved and the scouting movement might have become a major positive influence in my life, as it has been for my brother and my own three sons.

But as it turned out I never went back.

Perhaps I shouldn't be too critical. In later life I spent eighteen years or so as a voluntary youth worker and I know there were unguarded moments when I made unforgivable mistakes, perhaps with devastating results for some unfortunate youngster. If so I may one day become a focus of vitriol in the autobiography of a bitter and twisted Deepcar child. All I can say is that I had good intentions, did my best and not many others were willing to have a go.

A poor substitute for the scouts was the Play Centre, pronounced "Play Senner".

This took place in the school building, operated by the school teachers we had suffered all day, but instead of lessons we had a supposedly relaxing time. One room was full of old Dandies, Beanos, Toppers and so on. It would be true to say that Dennis the Menace was the hero on whom I modelled myself and the comics certainly helped develop my sense of humour.

Some of the back pages of the adventure comics opened up a whole new world of wonderment in the form of adverts by those masters of persuasion known as Ellisdons.

Adverts for Ellisdons products were guaranteed to encourage all the undesirable aspects of human nature. You could disgust your parents, amaze your friends, be the envy of your class mates and be the centre of attention. I'm ashamed to say I fell for some of the sales pitch. The first item I bought was a false thumb which looked as though it had been hit by a hammer. (Horrify your friends)

Next, for five shillings I bought a bird call which was guaranteed to imitate the call of any bird you could think of. It turned out to be a wooden tube with a metal insert which squeaked when turned. How exciting.

Not to be defeated I then bought a pack of indoor fireworks which was quite amusing for about half a minute.

After that I bought a crystal set which was advertised as a marvellous piece of modern technology containing a real germanium diode, producing radio broadcasts from all over the world without the need for batteries. It turned out to be a tiny plastic box with just a single transistor and a small coil inside, all visible because there was no back on the box.

Get Thi Neck Weshed

The impressive wavelength dial displayed on the advert turned out to be a paper sticker with a picture of a needle on. Incredibly, in a crude hissing and spluttering way, it actually worked without any batteries or power supply, but everything was in a foreign language, even the crackling. Thank god I learned sense before I got tempted by the Woopee Cushion (embarrass your dad) the Seebacroscope (spy on your neighbours) the throw your voice device (mystify your classmates) the imitation dog poo (get your dog an unjustified thrashing) the imitation soot (cause havoc in your sister's knicker drawer) and so on.

Unfortunately the teachers at play senner kept insisting that we did something more fulfilling than reading comics. They insisted on maintaining their control into our leisure time, and indeed into their own overtime! (Can you just imagine your pub landlord insisting, "That's enough darts you lot, get yourselves onto that pool table")

I remember doing the best painting I have ever done at play senner. It was a scene from the Plague of London and the duller the colours, the more ramshackle the buildings, the more messy the whole scene, the more realistic was the painting. It was just up my street.

All the bright colours which the other kids used for daisies and butterflies, when mixed together produced exactly the right shades of murky brown and grey to depict inner city, rat infested London in the 1660s.

I received the only accolade any of the Shepherd family ever had for art work.

What's more, the compliment was from no less a person than Mr. Wilson himself. (and believe me, there is no less a person than .....well you have got the message by now.)

Another time he insisted I did basket weaving and over a few weeks I made a beautiful picnic basket with a pretty design on the front. What kind of an achievement was that for a disciple of Dennis the Menace?

When I took it home I had to ask my mam for twelve and six for the materials.

She nearly fell through the floor as this was a tremendous amount of money to have to pay out unexpectedly from our meagre family income and the basket was about as appropriate in our house as my dad's fancy hearth rug and about as useful as a chocolate teapot.

Chapter Seven
'No sloggin' at Herries Road YM

For years before we joined the YM we used to play cricket on the pathway beside the building, using a dustbin as a wicket and the porch door as a wicket keeper.

My first experiences of the YMCA club on Herries Road were not of membership but as casual user of the outer premises. Having lost our field to the Five Arches pub, for years before we joined the YM we used to play cricket on the pathway beside the building, using a dustbin as a wicket and the porch door as a wicket keeper. The wall of the building was alongside the pitch so all strokes were to the right. (Is that silly mid off, or on or something?) otherwise you would risk being caught out with the "one hand off of t'wall" rule. Fortunately the windows were all covered in strong mesh.

A further restriction to the game was the "No Sloggin" rule which forbade anyone from hitting the ball too hard. Sometimes the batsman would be tempted by a sloppy ball and would slog the ball over the cars coming down Herries Road, thus accepting his fate under the "No sloggin, Six and Out" rule. When I think about it, there was hardly anywhere that it was possible or permissible to hit the ball at all.

The building was originally owned by the YWCA and along with its attached field, was known as "Wy Dubs." The YWCA logo stood proud on the end of the building and a street cred problem had to be overcome before me and Gus dared to join the YM under such an inappropriate emblem but we eventually put embarrassment aside.

Highlight of the evening at YM was toast and tea which everyone clamoured to prepare in the makeshift kitchen. For a penny more you could have a "crusty one" but for those not on duty, this required much cajoling as there were only two crusts per loaf (obviously.)

The massive room was heated by one pot bellied stove and a cast iron chimney, which could be seen to glow red when the stove was operated by a real expert (me). We had a small billiard table and the first one to arrive got a cue with a tip on. There was never any chalk but we didn't need it. All we had to do was reach up and chalk the cue from the dusty asbestos panels in the ceiling. I worry about that to this day but I am still okay up to now.

The club was run by Jim Lamb, and nobody was more aptly named. He was a small, thin blonde haired chap with a quiet voice and an evangelical smile. He must have felt like a missionary when he came into the estate and indeed he was. He never converted me to Christianity, which I presume was one of his objectives but he certainly had a lasting effect on me and I am not sure what direction my life might have taken if it were not for Jim and a few people like him.

He tried to get us involved in the running of the club and me and Gus were willing volunteers. From a sense of responsibility me and Gus once reported to him that Willie Bartram had not paid his subs – a major crime or so we thought.

Jim sat down with us in the office and told us what we already knew, that Willie was from a family with seven kids and no income. He had only one functioning lung and being not very robust did not have much of a social circle except for the youth club, which was the highlight of his life. In the end it was we, not Jim, who insisted that the matter of Willie's subs should be overlooked. What a crafty sod was Jim Lamb! But I'm glad now that we allowed Willie to enjoy his youth club days in peace as he died of natural causes a few years later.

On occasions Jim brought a helper with him to run the club. One such person called Alan came along regularly for a while. One day he announced half way through the session that his wallet had gone missing from his coat which was hung up in the kitchen.

All the lads rallied round trying to work out where it could be and one avenue of investigation was the young Downs Syndrome boy who had been in the kitchen for a while and then set off home a few minutes later. I regret to say that he was known to all and sundry as Mad Mick.

If Mick had possessed a tendency towards thieving the whole estate would have known about it for years and we didn't really suspect him, but nobody else had been in a situation to be suspected. Me and Gus thought he should be checked out and eliminated from our enquiries. When we caught up with him he was very confused about what we were asking and lost his temper with us but we were satisfied he didn't have the wallet.

On the next club night Alan called us all together, apologised for the false alarm and explained that his wallet had been found on his desk at work. He must have spent a whole week riddled with guilt. After he had bought double toast and tea for everyone in the club he was soon forgiven. In actual fact it could have happened to anybody and anyway he was a very nice bloke. His niceness prevailed throughout his life and he remained altruistic when his pewter business grew in leaps and bounds.

Eventually he became a millionaire but never forgot his roots or his interest in young people. In later life he was instrumental in supporting the well known Whirlow Farm Trust. His name was Alan Aitkin.

Behaviour in the youth club was far from subdued and Jim Lamb must have thought we were past redemption at times. The club was run largely on our terms but Jim did expect five minutes each night for what he referred to as "talk time" This consisted of club matters, a few moments of what one might call a sermon, and a very brief prayer. Nobody but Jim Lamb could get away with that on our estate.

During this time the local youth who were not club members would sometimes stand outside the windows jeering, making suggestive comments and generally interrupting Jim's important moment.

On one such occasion, heaven forbid, he showed just the slightest hint of human failing. He stopped what he was saying and instead he quietly said "OK lads, we've had enough of this. GET 'EM"

We charged out, shouting and cheering and chased the culprits in all directions around the estate. Most of us captured somebody and dragged them back into the club. I caught Rod Burgoine, a local lad much bigger and older than me, but he gave up meekly and I didn't have to fight him but led him back to the club hut holding his collar, which I could only just reach.

I can only assume that my divine inspiration and Rod's acquiescence were due to respect for Jim Lamb.

Me and Weedy wearing
Christmas presents, 1951

Another regular at the YM, I will call Weedy. He had been my best friend when we were younger.

When we had the prisoners surrounded in the middle of the room and Jim asked "Right lads, what shall we do with them" I don't think he was prepared for the detailed anatomical suggestions we came up with. My own proposal, that we hang them, was the most moderate suggestion of the night and in that atmosphere on that night I'm sure we would have done it if Jim had not returned to his normal placid, forgiving self and promoted the unheard of notion of forgiveness.

Thankfully he didn't suggest praying for them or there would have been a full scale rebellion.

Rod Burgoine was not hanged and survived my vindictive intentions. After that we had a mutual respect for each other until unfortunately he died quite suddenly of an un-diagnosed heart complaint before he reached his early twenties. Perhaps he was always physically unfit. Perhaps I was not so tough after all.

Another regular at the YM, I will call Weedy. He had been my best friend when we were younger. His dad worked for the railways, always wore his crumpled uniform proudly and never took his pipe-full of Condor Twist out of his mouth. He had a hearing aid which was as big as a Glastonbury amplifier but it didn't work well even on the rare occasions that he turned it on.

Mrs. Weedy was the female equivalent of Mr. Weedy, except that her hearing aid was bigger and worked. She had a permanent grin on her face which was more to do with her false teeth than her mood.

Weedys were the first family on our street to get a television, indeed theirs was a very popular house on Coronation Day. Me and Weedy loved to go and watch their telly despite his dad getting irritated with our presence. I often wonder why people have kids when they don't like them. If I fidgeted too much he would look irritated but say nothing. Instead he would wait ages for his boy Weedy to do something similar then he would shout "Keep still will you!"

Television was a serious business in those days and led to ancillary products such as TV biscuits, TV trays etc.

The telly was viewed with the room lights turned off, which led to the invention of the so called TV Lamp. This was an ordinary reading lamp placed right on top of the television in the worst conceivable place.

Just in case anyone could still see the picture, Weedy's dad invested in colour television decades before the real thing was invented.

His consisted of a sheet of plastic over the screen, which was shaded blue on top, clear in the middle and I think, green on the bottom.

How gullible can one get? The combined effects of the coloured screen, a haze of Condor smoke and the badly placed TV lamp produced the most unsuitable circumstances imaginable for watching a nine inch black and white telly.

If there was ever a hope of seeing the picture properly a car would go past with no suppressor fitted and the old familiar flecking pattern would dance across the screen until the noise of the engine faded away up Herries Road.

Anyway a telly was a telly and it was many years before we Shepherds joined the telly owning classes.

Old Coultas was not the only one to get knocked down on "our" zebra crossing.

One day Weedy was coming back from the chip shop and was knocked flying by a car as he crossed the road. Mr. Belisha and his ridiculous beacon invention have a lot to answer for and I am sure that most accidents to pedestrians must occur on Zebra Crossings.

Anyway Weedy was not hurt very much and it fell upon his mother to summarise the seriousness of his situation, with a phrase which she repeated all around the estate for years to come, and I quote :-

"And he lost all his chips!"

Due to the one year difference in our age, Weedy and I spent less time together in later years but there was always a bond of friendship between us. He was a bit wild and started mixing with lads three or four years older than us. I will never forget the Saturday morning as I lay in bed my mother called upstairs.

"Graham. I've got a shock for you. Weedy's been killed."

Although I had come across death before, this unforgettable moment was the first time that I had felt bereavement like a knife deep in my soul.

Sometimes my leisure activities led to trouble. On one occasion me and my mate Not David went into Dicko's Wood during dinner break and were playing with matches.

The circumstances were typical of events which appear all too regularly in newspapers today. A boy of sixteen was pleased to get an apprenticeship as a motor mechanic and quickly became so trusted that he knew where to find the workshop keys and keys to a car he had been working on. Temptation and the opportunity to gain street cred overcame him and the result was an illicit trip up Rivelin Valley with three pals, plus my much younger treasured mate Weedy.

An elderly couple coming the other way were injured. Two boys had several broken limbs. Another boy, known locally as Crazy Keith, was so smashed up that for several weeks he pleaded to be allowed to die - a strikingly undignified reaction from a lad who had never before had a serious thought in his young head.

But only eternal silence from my old friend Weedy.

Following that tragedy a girl next-door-but-one who always had a weak heart finally faded away. Some time later a lad from the prefabs down the road died after being struck on the temple by a stone from a catapult. He was a bit of a quiet lad who didn't mix and the lad responsible was somewhat notorious but I don't know enough of the facts to make judgements. All I can say is, if life were preserved at the cost of all else, lads would not be lads.

Around that time the oldest of the Rickie boys (They of the Rickie Hat fame and mentioned again later) was tragically killed by something literally and ironically, falling off the back of a lorry. This along with the deaths of Rod and Willie brought the score to six young deaths within a hundred yards radius. I was lucky to get off the estate alive.

Sometimes my leisure activities led to trouble. On one occasion me and my mate Not David went into Dicko's Wood during dinner break and were playing with matches. We set a few bits of grass on fire and eventually we (If I'm honest it was "I" not "we") set fire to an old, dry privet hedge with tall dry grass growing through it.

With hearts in mouths and butterflies in stomachs we made futile attempts to beat the fire out but it quickly became an inferno. Soon, to make matters worse we heard the distant sound of the school bell ringing.

We decided to run like hell and with sooty faces and singed hair we managed to get inside the school gates half a mile away (where we had actually been all the time-honest!) just as the fire engine clanged up Herries Road towards the massive pall of smoke which was clearly visible over the allotments in Dicko's Wood.

Don't ever let anyone tell you that young people brag about this kind of thing and enjoy the street cred amongst their contemporaries.

What perpetrators of this kind of crime do, in truth, is to never sleep again, swear each other to secrecy and never breathe a word about it again until they write a book in their dotage when they think it might be safe. I hope that the new developments with DNA and the recent police inclination for cold case reviews do not lead to the awakening of the fifty year long mystery – Who set fire to Dicko's Wood?

Another unhappy event in Dicko's Wood involved a local lad I will call Dimmie, which was not his name. (Are you getting the idea?) He was older and bigger than us and was a bit nutty.

His favourite greeting was a cross between a Tarzan call and the reply of the gorilla which Tarzan was calling. In fact he resembled the gorilla in appearance and mannerism. Just to give you an idea of his intelligence, his main hobby was collecting house numbers.

He would go up each path with his little notebook and write down, say, 82 then up the next path and write 84 and so on. I wonder if he ever noticed the emerging mathematical sequence.

Anyway Dimmie used to follow me and Gus about and we tolerated him sometimes but when we were fed up of him we would play Hiddy until it was his turn to be "on" then we would just run miles away and leave him, eyes pressed into forearm, struggling to count to a hundred.

It would be days before we saw him again, by which time he had either forgiven us or assumed that he was just rubbish at playing Hiddy.

(I am now thoroughly ashamed of this kind of behaviour by the way.)

But on the day in question some sort of rough and tumble started

I am in full agreement with those people who advise us never to pick on people smaller than ourselves, but surely it would be much more sensible to advise us not to pick on those a lot bigger and shaped like a gorilla.

between me and Dimmie and it kind of slowly got rougher and tumbler until a proper fight resulted.

He was much too big for me and I ended up with bruises all over. I am in full agreement with those people who advise us never to pick on people smaller than ourselves, but surely it would be much more sensible to advise us not to pick on those a lot bigger and shaped like a gorilla.

When my dad came home and saw my beaten up appearance he just assumed that I had been bullied or attacked, which was not really how it happened.

If ever my dad went into a confrontation he made a point of keeping his factory clothes and chin stubble on, which was his normal state anyway, in an attempt to look hard. So out he went, dragging me with him, to explain to Mr. Dimmie senior that he should learn to control the behaviour of young Dimmie junior.

Going down their path we were met by young Dimmie coming up, also their massive Alsatian. Unperturbed by the dog, my dad marched us all into the house, where Dimmie senior went into defence mode and explained the difficulties involved in trying to bring up a difficult boy all alone with no woman to help. (Mrs. Dimmie was in Middlewood Asylum.)

Mr. Dimmie was both plausible and pitiable. He expressed his plight more eloquently than an expert sociologist could have done. He sympathised and apologised profusely for the unfortunate situation that had arisen between me and his normally manageable son.

My dad accepted the apology and backed off. It is amazing how persuasive a well conducted reasonable argument can be when presented by a man trying to hold back a snarling Alsatian. We came away almost in tears.

The last I heard of Dimmie, he was running his own window cleaning

Two other rather strange girls lived on the same street. One was called King Wello after her habit of wearing Wellington boots day in, day out, all year long.

business and probably earning twice as much as me. Good luck to him. Despite our pointless fight he was never a vindictive person and did not have a very good start in life. I am relieved to know that he is not still searching the streets of Sheffield 5 shouting

"All in, all out, last man gets a clout."

Dimmie managed to get through life without the help of the authorities but there were others who could have done with a bit of guidance.

For example there was a girl I will call Aggie who seemed unable to keep herself clean and looked very undernourished. She went around talking loudly to everybody especially any unfortunate bus passenger who was careless enough to have an empty seat nearby.

She ended up with four or five kids before she reached twenty and every one was a different colour. Each father in turn was the real love of her life at last and they were going to get married.

Another nameless young woman would wonder around the shops clearly irritated by an entourage of kids around her, which she would curse, threaten and remonstrate with all day long to get them to behave. This was not an unusual situation in our area but in her case it was complicated by the fact that there were no kids there at all except in her imagination.

I used to wonder if her children had been taken away.

There was obviously a very sad story behind her circumstances.

Two other rather strange girls lived on the same street. One was called King Wello after her habit of wearing Wellington boots day in, day out, all year long.

I have no idea why King and not Queen, but one didn't look for logic in these situations. King Wello's friend was called Swearbugger for obvious reasons.

I am no expert on Tourettes syndrome but I believe it involves spontaneous outbursts. In the case of Swearbugger it was not a series

Boys' games got very violent and even a potentially innocent game such as Ball Tiggy was taken to extremes. Sometimes a rock hard "corky" ball was used

of outbursts, more a continuous stream of swearwords shouted loudly at anyone within earshot, morning till night.

Swearwords with more than two or three syllables would have another swearword inserted in the middle for extra dramatic effect.

Anyway, enough of the rich tapestry of life on the streets of Sheffield 5.

Let us move to the relative normality within the school gates.

Schoolyard games followed a strict annual pattern.

Conkers and "slairing" on the ice were obviously seasonal. (An exception applied to kids with big hobnail boots who could slair all the rest of the year but were banned from ice slairs because their boots spoiled the slair.) But other games, for no obvious reason, followed a strict calendar which must be genetically embedded in the instincts of children.

Boys' games got very violent and even a potentially innocent game such as Ball Tiggy was taken to extremes. Sometimes a rock hard "corky" ball was used and if a victim was cornered all he could do was curl up into the foetal position and take a merciless blow in the kidneys. He was then "on" and if he could still stand up he would stagger around in an attempt to catch a victim for himself.

Another violent game was called "Finger, Fum or a Rustybum" One team would kneel down in a line against the wall clutching each other's waist. The other team would take turns to leap along the line as far as possible and land on the row of backbones trying not to fall off. If the game progressed to its conclusion there would be team 2 balanced on the backs of team 1 and the front man in team 1 would stick out a finger, thumb or fist and ask the lead jumper of team 2 to guess "finger, fum or a rustybum."

That was the theory. In actual fact the game rarely progressed to this point. The jumper always tried to jump high and land hard with his knees in the kidneys of one of the crouching forms.

Tactics played an important part. Lightly built lads were good jumpers

Me and Gus in later years at Skeggy, taken
by a persuasive street photographer

but didn't kill the opponent when they landed. Big fat lads landed heavily but tended to wobble and fall off the line. When a seriously injured victim in the line collapsed in agony his last breath would be spent in proclaiming that the jumper had fallen off, whilst the jumper would complain bitterly that it was a "collapse."

If by some fluke the game and its players survived to the end, the jumper had a one in three chance of being correct with his guess of finger, fum or rustybum. However the chances of his opponent admitting that the guess was correct and able to prove it with finger or fum still attached to his hand, would be more like a million to one against.

Me and my mate Gus were almost inseparable for years. At first his mam didn't approve because she was a little bit snooty and she didn't want him mixing with the wrong crowd, meaning me. She thought I was "too rough" and might lead their Gus into trouble, which I did at every opportunity. Despite this, in later years our two families became good friends.

Gus's dad was a bit of a character. He used to call us the "Don't Know Gang." because whenever he asked us where we were going or what we were doing he got the same curt reply. "Don't Know." Usually we did know but there was no way we were going to tell him.

He was a saw doctor at Spear and Jackson and he had the typical dry factory humour appreciated by nobody else in the world outside of Sheffield.

I remember one day we wanted to go to the pictures and Gus went to his dad, saying,

"Dad, can I lend (meaning borrow) half a crown?"

"Eye lad, it just so 'appens I keep half a crown specially for lending out to people who need it in an emergency."

Our little faces lit up then he said,

"It's out at the moment and I can't remember where, but if ever it comes back I will let you have it straight away."

With a perfectly straight face he went back to his Daily Mirror sports page. However after a bit more tormenting he relented and we got the loan.

At one time me and Gus made the biggest and best trolley in the world. It was the usual hand propelled, pram wheels, shoe sole brake, rope or foot steering, plank axle design but the main platform was pure polished

They unveiled a monster trolley which had lorry seats and a lorry steering wheel. It was very impressive but not very practical.

walnut veneer because it was made from the top of a discarded piano. One day I crashed into a concrete post going down the steep part of Herries Road by Scraith Wood and I still believe I broke my ankle but it was left to get better by itself, which took several months.

Some time later we were outdone by the Rickie brothers, they of the Rickie Hat craze. They unveiled a monster trolley which had lorry seats and a lorry steering wheel. It was very impressive but not very practical. Not surprising as it was fundamentally a lorry. It took two to push it on the flat and one to push it down hill.

After that we downsized our mode of transport and took to "trazzing" down Barrie Crescent sitting on a small square of board laid across an old roller skate. The deluxe version had a square of old carpet on top. Snobbery was alive and well in Parson Cross. Steering was achieved (or not) by leaning from side to side, and stopping was achieved (or not) by the simple act of rolling off.

Gus was not allowed a bike because his Mam said they are dangerous. This called for a cunning plan and cunning plans were what we were good at. The answer was for Gus to have no bike and for me to have two. We acquired a smallish bike frame from somewhere and married it up to parts from a very ancient and abandoned oversized tandem. It had massive wheels with drum brakes, big thick cables and ridiculously high gear ratios. If I remember rightly there was also a dynamo in one of the hubs. We named it "The Tank". It was so bulky that a reverse gear would have been handy. It was only missing a motor bike engine and I'm sure it would have been suitable for a side car. It weighed a ton, was as ugly as sin and was totally impractical but it served a purpose.

One day we were coming down from t'Forum and went two abreast round the traffic island at Shercliff Road. A bloke in a big posh car came up behind us hooting and eventually pulled us over, yelling,

"What do you think you are doing going two abreast round the island? I couldn't get past."

Quite often I would forget to say where I was going or when I was coming back and I'm not sure if my absence was even noticed for ages

I replied that there was nothing in the Highway Code to say that riding two abreast was wrong.

Having just passed my cycling proficiency test I was an expert and ready for a frank and interesting exchange of views but all the pompous prat could say was

"Do you know who I am?"

Unfortunately I am not the type to fall on my knees and worship people who are important especially when their importance doesn't extend beyond their own inflated ego, so I replied

"Yes, you are the bloke who thinks it is OK to overtake two young cyclists on a traffic island."

With that, he thought for a while, got back in his car and drove away. He probably realised that his fancy car would have come nowhere in a battle with "The Tank."

The bikes enabled me and Gus to go "tracking" in Beeley Woods or take sandwiches and five Park Drive Tipped for days out up Rivelin Valley. Quite often I would forget to say where I was going or when I was coming back and I'm not sure if my absence was even noticed for ages, but when I arrived home the familiar cry would meet me as I crept indoors trying not to draw attention to myself – a difficult task in a small house in pre-television days. The cry would go out.

"Weers tha been while nar?"

Grammar was not high priority at the Shepherd house.

My return was evidence that all the dangers that could befall a young lad had not in fact occurred, so I was never in big trouble about it.

Sometimes the "Weers Tha been" was followed by another remark,

"Tha' worse than thi dad." and I'm sure similar conversations must have occurred back in the annals of Shepherd history and will continue into the distant future throughout Parson Cross and Shercliff.

These recollections inspired the following poem, which will bring me fame and fortune any day now.

Chapter Eight
Weers Tha Been While Nar?

N a, mi father was a grinder in
a Sheffield penknife works
And a little bit of overtime
was one of his few perks
But though he worked till eight at
neet to earn his extra pay
He got home well past eleven to
hear my mother say,
Weers tha been while nar, -
Weers tha been while nar.

Tha's only earned a bob or two with
workin' extra late
And tha's spent about a fiver in that
pub at factory gate
Tha's chucked away thi money
over't Mailcoach bar
Why dun't tha admit it. That's weer
tha's been while nar

When I were a little lad I played wi
our dog Gyp
We'd wade right over't river Don
then jump off Shercliff tip
I got muddier and bloodier and
filthier and wetter
And went home late in a sorry state
– and Gyp was not much better
Weers tha been while nar –
Weers tha been while nar

Get them mucky clothes off and get
stood in that sink
And save thi watter for that dog,
he's causing a reight stink
What's that on thi trousers? Oh. no
it looks like tar
It's ages past thy bedtime.
Weers tha been while nar.

Then I grew to be a teenager. I
joined that Mojo Club
I got myself a girlfriend - and a
Triumph Tiger Cub!
We'd rock and Roll a little then ride
off till God knows when
Then I'd burn home for my
reprimand. (Watches didn't have
digits then.)

Weer's tha been while nar –
Weers tha been while nar.

We're worried to death about thee
and we don't like motor bikes
And it seems to us just lately that
tha just does what tha likes
We said tha could stop out till twelve
and that would be OK
But let's be reight about it, we
meant twelve O'clock same day!

Get Thi Neck Weshed

But now, I've got quite settled
down, I've got more simple needs
A pint of Stones on Friday night,
then fish and chips and peas
But when I take 'em home wi' me,
my pleasure starts to fade
As I get to our front door to be met
wi't wife's tirade

Weer's tha been while nar.
Weer tha been while nar
Out wi' all thi' mate agean down at
Lowoods Club
And coming home at this time wi' thi
parcel full of grub
I can see tha's not brought me
none, No cos tha't too tight
Well enjoy thi' fish and chips lad
- cos it's all tha'll get tonight!

So I open up my chips and I'm
sitting down to dine

When I hear't front door latch
clicking. It's that young lad o'mine
He's later than his father, now surely
that's not reight
But when I start to tell him off, I can't
keep my face straight

Weer's tha been while nar.
Weers tha been while nar

He sees my eyes a twinkling, I'm not
angry he can tell
Then we both collapse in laughter
as in unison we yell

Weer tha been while nar.
Weers tha been while nar

Was it like this when I was young?
Eye lad - of course it war
Here, have a chip - Come tell thy
dad where tha's been while nar.

Weapons played a part in every boy's life. In our tender years the
favourite was the humble pea shooter. We used to cut a stem from the
plant ominously known as Motherdie.
(I am not superstitious but I cannot help observing that most of the
mothers of people who cut the plant have now died.) If dried peas were
not available we would use hawthorn berries. It was a long time before we
realised that the horrible painful inflammation we got on our lips were due
to the poisonous acidic nature of sap of this particular weed. Don't try
this at home kids.
Another weapon we developed was the frameless catapult which could
not be detected by a quick body search. If you get six strong elastic
bands strung together with finger-loops on each end and a sling in the

centre made from an elastoplast, the result is an extremely powerful catapult. I would not recommend that my young readers get involved in this type of activity.

If you do, you could be tempted to fire a dried pea in unsuitable surroundings, such as the Kids Christmas Concert at Southey Club. It could hit somebody like, just for instance, Phil Hopley, right on the end of the nose and he, and you, would be very lucky that he didn't lose an eye. Phil Hopley might be quite a mate of yours and even though he doesn't know who it was to this day because it is hard to look around with your eyes watering and your nose bleeding, you will know yourself that it was you and you will feel guilty for decades to come. Seriously, don't try this at home kids.

Once in Beeley Woods a detective in a Morris Minor saw me with an air pistol in my pocket. He assumed I was shooting birds, which I would never do (though I did once shoot a rat in the River Don). He nicked me for being under age in charge of a firearm. To our total shame and embarrassment he came to the house whilst Posh Uncle Ken and Aunty Rose were there to Sunday tea and my sins were paraded before them. The detective tried to negotiate that if the gun was given up for destruction there would be no further action but my dad insisted that it be given back, after all it cost twenty five bob, so the detective went away saying that he would be back as soon as the prosecution report had been processed.

After what seemed like a lifetime of waiting we saw my mate Dicteen's dad (The police desk officer at Hammerton Road) and my dad asked him if anything had happened at the station such as a bottle of ink spilling over a certain report with my name on it. He just laughed and said with a wink, "Well, accidents like that can happen sometimes you know." Throughout the "arrest" Gus had an identical pistol in his pocket as well but the copper never noticed.

After the incident Gus was not allowed to keep his air pistol any more so he gave it to me. I had two and he had none. It doesn't take a genius to work out that on average this worked out at one gun each and the status quo was re-established.

The cunning plan had worked again.

In fairness I can understand why the police didn't want youngsters roaming about with air guns. I myself had once been shot at close range with a powerful .22 rifle.

In fairness I can understand why the police didn't want youngsters roaming about with air guns. I myself had once been shot at close range with a powerful .22 rifle. It was aimed at a tree I was leaning on but this only served to flatten and sharpen the pellet enabling it to glance off and penetrate deep into my thigh.

Events like this were accepted as normal hazards of the world of childhood and I don't think I even told my parents what had happened. For some reason kids at that time lived with an in-built guilt complex and assumed they would be in serious trouble for doing something as ill disciplined as getting shot.

I must say that with the exception of Dicteen's dad I held the police in low esteem. This stemmed from an experience which occurred when I was very small and impressionable. It was a rare occasion; we had been to see my Aunty in Cleethorpes on a train and walked back up Pond Street late on Saturday night. Outside a pub a big crowd had gathered, something had obviously occurred, trouble was in the air and the police were out in force.

One copper walked straight across the road to the crowd and smacked a man hard in the face for no apparent reason, knocking him into an old lady who was so small and frail that she reminded me of Old Mother Riley. She went down flat with the victim of the assault on top of her until he was dragged off and thrown into the "Black Maria." For all I know he might have been a mass murderer but I only saw what I saw, and my bitterness towards the police stayed with me well into adulthood.

One of our favourite places to hang around was the playground at Longley. It had the usual rocking horse, swings and roundabout which were no fun at all when played with properly but very entertaining when misused. Best of all was the Flying Plank which when full of kids weighed about a ton. It swung to and fro, end on, like a pendulum and any child (or even an elephant for that matter) walking too near to an end would have

One evening per week this served as the forerunner of a phenomenon known as the discotheque but without the lights, amplification or atmosphere.

been killed outright. It is unbelievable that deaths did not occur every day. Cast iron stops limited the plank's movement to prevent it from launching itself over the horizon and our objective was to get it "up to't bumpers" when at the end of its swing the plank stopped abruptly whilst us kids continued, crashing our delicate parts against the iron loops onto which we clung. Strange what passed for pleasure in Longley Play ground.

In a nearby hut there was a uniformed keeper with an officious cap called Owd Jackson (The keeper, not the cap) whose job it was to come out and yell at little kids for no reason, a task which he sometimes undertook with the utmost enthusiasm.

Fortunately his second favourite pastime was sitting in the hut out of sight so that he didn't have to see us. Also as a council employee he seemed to be off sick for precisely thirteen weeks every year. All this is a far cry from our modern Park Rangers who get involved in education, woodland maintenance and the care of the largest area of City woodland in Europe. But again I digress.

Next to the Longley playground there was a prefabricated hut called the "British Legion". One evening per week this served as the forerunner of a phenomenon known as the discotheque but without the lights, amplification or atmosphere.

Kids would just take turns to put scratchy records on an old record player. Boys and girls four or five years older than me would dress themselves up and put themselves about, making dramatic entrances with statements like "I've come and to prove it I'm here" and asking each other "You dancin?" "You askin" etc. I sometimes went with our Norma.

On reflection I must have been quite a burden to her but I can't recall any resentment. Perhaps taking me along made it easier for her to get permission and the entrance fee from our dad.

The organiser of the event was Owd Meakin. If you think of an appropriate young lively jive talkin' fun lovin' hip hoppin' gig promoter and

We realised there and then there were professions even more exciting than train driving or bus driving.

then try to imagine a character from the opposite end of that spectrum, and then go further in the same direction for a very long time, you will still not arrive at Owd Meakin. He was obviously an old wounded soldier, slightly disfigured and blind.

Whether he was raising funds for the Legion, the blind or just earning a crust in the only way he could, I don't know, but without him the youngsters of the district would have had one less thing to occupy them of an evening. I was too young for that type of event but I came in handy sometimes. I remember once, after an evening at the Legion, Ronnie Fairfax gave me a genuine ex army jack knife just for going to ask our Norma if she would have a word with him at our front gate.

One of the most constructive activities I indulged in was swimming. The initial interest arose from school swimming lessons. With heavy woollen trunks rolled into our towels we would all traipse off onto the Shercliff bus, where we would be enthralled if the ticket machine was one of the paper roll type and the teacher was presented with a big long roll which we would beg for, shouting.

"Sir, can I have it sir, he had it last week sir, it's my turn sir, sir, sir, sir."

We would then get off at the Wicker Arches and walk along the narrow streets past all the factories to Corporation Street baths alias "Copo"

On one occasion as we walked along the back streets we were fascinated to see one of the big factory doors open up and some men came out with big oil drums and planks which they placed across the road to form a barrier. Inside, a red hot steel bar was snaking across the floor and as a team of men, biting onto sweat towels, manipulated it with big tongs, it grew thinner and longer until it came out of the door, over the pavement and finally reached half way across the road.

We stood behind the makeshift barrier with mouths wide open at the sight and we realised there and then there were professions even more exciting than train driving or bus driving.

However I was mindful of the man with a wooden leg who lived somewhere around Galsworthy Road.

Me and Weedy in Rivelin paddling pool

No wonder we learned to swim a length after only a week or two. The only difficulty was jumping in without hitting dry land at the other end.

The legend was that one day in a rolling mill a red hot rod of steel went through his leg and all his mates could do was hold him up and wait until it had all passed through. The story might not be true – I hope it isn't. When we reached the baths we would have to queue outside until another school charged out looking all pink faced, red eyed and etched clean with no need to get their necks weshed for the rest of the week. Swimming time was valuable and the time spent in the queue was not to be wasted.

We would stand in the street undoing shoe laces, unbuttoning shirts, taking arms out of shirt and vest sleeves, undoing snake belts and sometimes taking socks off and stuffing them into pockets. Some kids had trunks already on underneath trousers, another ten seconds saved. A cheer would then start at the front of the queue and work to the back like a Mexican wave as we all charged in half undressed, shirts flapping and struggling to hold our trousers up with one hand whilst holding a rolled up towel under the other arm.

Some of the lads seemed to be in the cubicle for a matter of seconds before they bombed into the water to the annoyance of Frank, the bath attendant who sometimes swam naked in between the swimming sessions for reasons known only to him.

So that was the humble place where I and thousands like me learned to swim. If you go and look at the site now you will still see a few white tiles in the remaining foundations but you will be incredulous that such a small area could have housed a swimming baths. No wonder we learned to swim a length after only a week or two. The only difficulty was jumping in without hitting dry land at the other end.

Sometimes me and Phil Hopley would go swimming by ourselves on Saturday mornings. The first step was to apply for Bath tickets which were issued by the Education Office. These were simple squares torn from a perforated card, each bearing the one uncomplicated word, SCHOLAR. Bath tickets became part of schoolyard currency along with

After a few minutes privately guessing the weight of customers using the old brass beam scales we would then walk round to Bunneys

red plastic bus tokens, which could be swapped for sweets, conkers or mabs. In a similar way, adults would sometimes use Banner checks or milk checks as coins of the realm.

One day at the baths me and Phil were getting dried when Frank the attendant came around kicking the cubicle doors open and when he saw I had still got my trunks on he ordered me to take them off then he just stood there staring at me until I did so, then for an uncomfortable while after. I don't know what his game was but I felt very embarrassed and I'm sure that if a bath attendant did that today it would be a significant if concluding moment in his career.

After swimming we would walk back to town via the brewery on Bridge Street, from which there came a wonderful malty smell of brewing beer which dominated the Castlegate area. I was almost adult before I ever questioned what the smell was. As a child I just thought that was how town smelled. (A bit like the Queen believing that the whole world smells of fresh paint!) Before getting on the bus we would often divert to the Rag Market where we would go into the old ramshackle building to look at all the animals and listen to a man shouting, "Whoooos rabbit buyin' pigeon buyin' budgie buyin.'"

After a few minutes privately guessing the weight of customers using the old brass beam scales we would then walk round to Bunneys, have a quick look at the teddy boy clothes in the window and then go into the fish market where we would buy a plate of whelks for threppence before going to Castlegate bus stop and home, contented, on the number 63, still chewing the whelks until half way up Cooks Wood Road.

Saturday mornings down town were magical compared with the clinical characterless world of Meadowhall. So nostalgic are the memories that one day when my wife and I set off to make some purchases our destination was still in debate when we got to the junction where the decision had to be made. I got out-voted but by the time we got home the following poem was almost complete in my mind.

Meadowhall

They don't have whelks in
Meadowhall. They're nowhere to be
seen
I've searched in every corner every
time I've been
They've got Kentucky Chicken, and
Mac Fries with fizzy pop
But there's not a whelk in
Meadowhall. I've asked in every
shop.

It's not like down the market, where
they sell you what you need
Like cracked eggs at knock down
prices, when you've hungry mouths
to feed
If you want that kind of purchase,
you've to get them off the shelf
And pay a silly price for them, and
crack the sods yourself

The women wave their mobile
phones and credit cards about
Designer labels showing. (Do they
wear them inside out?)
They curse their little offspring and
threaten them with a smack
But when they lose them in the
crowd, they want the buggers back.

Years ago on that same site, all

household goods were free
Brushes, tools and toilet rolls, all
there for you and me
But then this "horn of plenty" came
to a sudden stop
When they went and knocked the
steelworks down and changed it to
a shop.

But to leave a good reminder to be
viewed by you and I
They've made some big bronze
statues of those steelworks days
gone by
They've really caught the attitude of
workers of the past
And they've certainly got the speed
right – they're not moving very fast
And are they really casting ingots?
Look closely and you'll see,
They're either nicking scrap or
mashing giant pots of tea.

No, you can't get whelks in
Meadowhall, no udder or cow heel
No chitterlings, bag or chap bone
for an economic meal
No winkles, tripe or beast cheek, no
bacon bones at all
But it has a super Supertram–it goes
straight to't market hall.

Edible treats after swimming were part of the ritual.

Jim Lamb of YMCA fame used to take us swimming at Glossop Road and near the end of the session he used to throw loose change into the water and we would dive for it. The incentive was strong and to this day I can swim better under water with my eyes open than I can on top. The objective was to collect enough money for the back street chip shop on the way home. Egon Ronay could not find words to adequately describe the unique onion flavoured rissoles produced by that modest establishment near Glossop Road.

It occurs to me that I am experienced enough to produce a Rough Guide to Swimming Baths and Apres Swim Eating Establishments. It would look something like this.

Baths	Comments	Food nearby
Sutherland Rd. (Suds)	Concentrated Chlorine	None
Longley (Outdoor)	Bloody freezing Knot hole view to girls cubicles	Hurleys ice cream (Fog in it)
Hillsbro'	Good	Broken biscuits on Holme Lane
Glossop Rd.	Building Falling down	Rissoles to die for
Corporation St. (Copo)	Watch out for Bent Frank.	Whelks (Market Hall)

I could make a fortune with this idea except that none of the places are still open. Don't it make you feel old?

Chapter Nine
'Daan't medders'

Wardsend Cemetery. Scene of blackberry picking, war games and dark deeds

Much of my leisure time was spent "daan t'medders" which was the general term for Wardsend and Parkwood Springs. This area had everything a child could ask for. One might assume that an ash tip in the middle of a so-called meadow would spoil the area but in actual fact it was a real asset. Most of the tip was flat on top but in some areas separate lorry loads formed an ideal "tracking" area. Tracking was the art of riding a bike up and down hilly ground with the handle bars turned up like cow horns. In later years I tried it on my motor bike and I am sure it would be a major recreational asset if it were there today, but for reasons unknown the powers that be decided to spend a decade or two removing it completely and another decade or two putting it back again, but this time comprised of less desirable material.

If we came across an old enamel advertising sign (now collectable and worth a fortune) or a hearth plate we would slide down the tip side at breakneck speed.

The sides of the tip were angled at about 45 degrees and great fun could be had using old oil drums and other rubbish to build a barricade at the bottom, then rolling discarded lorry tyres down to crash into the blockade. If we came across an old enamel advertising sign (now collectable and worth a fortune) or a hearth plate we would slide down the tip side at breakneck speed.

If nothing else was available we would just run and jump off the edge of the tip and travel through the air for perhaps thirty feet or more before landing at such a sharp angle in the loose ash that we were unscathed but half buried in the sulphurous smelly stuff.

We would arrive home late, tired, bedraggled and filthy to the core. It was the kind of muck that hid under the skin and re-emerged after washing. It was a definite case of "And get thi neck weshed!"

My poor old mam would have to take over the situation and try to get me clean enough for school the next day. Fortunately the required standard was not that high.

Another favourite playing spot was the old barracks on Shercliff top, known variously as t' Barracks, t' Gunsights or t' Squatter's Huts, but nicknamed Barrackio by me and Gus.

It was here that during the war the brave British Army or was it the Home Guard made themselves inconspicuous by shining their big searchlight into the sky, presumably to let the German bombers know where they were, whilst everyone else had to turn their lights off and hide.

The neglected site itself was nothing short of paradise to young lads. There were several huts, all open with various rooms, lofts and cupboards to hide in. Outdoors there were concrete tunnels, channels and an ammunition dump, empty of course. There are still some gun foundations and trackways left for the nostalgic to peruse.

There was one building in good repair which housed a family with two young boys.

One day they told their dad that me and Gus were playing in the huts. He came out and found us in a water tank in the rafters of one of the huts and after giving us a lecture he confiscated my catapult then threatened to call the police. This was a bit of a relief because he was always dressed in some sort of black uniform himself and until then was believed to be a copper.

Bristling with success after the chip shop wall incident I declared that I would send the police myself because he had stolen my catapult. Once again courage won the day and the catapult was returned.

Years later the site was flattened and changed into Sheffield Heliport and a prime playground for the kids of Shercliff was lost.

Now the thing about heliports is that in order to be useful they need to attract passing helicopters and there never were any so the scheme was never going to be a success.

Last remnant of barracks, gunsights and searchlight post on Shercliff Top

Another excellent play area lost for ever was the land between Wordsworth Avenue and Cookson Road. There used to be a nice little deep valley with trees, hawthorn bushes and a stream in the bottom, a perfect mirror image of the nearby Scraith Wood. It was ideal for playing cowboys or hiddy and we used to have war games, shooting hawthorn berries at each other with pea shooters, catapults or even air pistols. A direct hit was marked with a red splodge, sometimes berry juice, sometimes blood.

We must have been the originators of the now popular paint balling craze. If only our inventiveness had been backed up with business acumen we would be millionaires now.

One day the council in its wisdom decided at great expense to culvert the stream, fill the whole valley in and lay tarmac on top. And what was the intended use of this featureless flat landscape? I think you can guess-a children's playground of course.

Much more recently I see that the area is grassed over and a proper playground has been installed. To be fair, it does look as if it is quite popular.

Another attraction down't medders was Wardsend Cemetery which, thanks to the "Friends of Wardsend Cemetery" is at least as enchanting today as it was then, except that in those days the chapel was still standing, derelict and of course, haunted. Well it had to be didn't it. Those occupying the graves did not need to progress any further as the graveyard was heaven itself. One could ride, run, play hiddy, shoot catapults, fail to catch lizards, smoke dad's dog ends, eat blackberries or just wander around reading the inscriptions on the graves, which date from the seventeen hundreds to the nineteen fifties. It was fascinating to observe the short life expectancy, the size of families and the infant mortality in times gone by.

Regrettably some of the gravestones also had some contemporary inscriptions on the back, written in chalk. Whilst the spelling was erratic, some of the biological information was quite accurate and very educational especially when supported by diagrams.

I won't elaborate further except to say that it substituted quite well for the lack of sex education at Shercliff school.

On one occasion word went around that one of the big vaults in Wardsend Cemetery had been broken open and human skulls thrown around. One skull was arrested and put in the cell in Hammerton Road which had earlier housed our budgie. Dicteen's dad said that several of the hardened coppers at Hammerton Road would not go near it at any price despite its impeccable behaviour.

One of my classmates, Patrick Rafferty (a classmate on the few occasions that he attended) returned to the scene of the crime with some other lads and whilst larking about, threw an axe which he just happened to have with him, (as you do). It nearly hit a plain clothed policeman who happened to be hiding in the bushes nearby (as they do).

After that, Patrick left our class for a while to be educated in a place more suited to his particular lifestyle. It was a place he had visited on previous occasions after expressing his individuality in ways which society didn't appreciate. I don't know what became of him, he wasn't a friend of mine but to me he seemed quite a likeable character with a big Irish grin and friendly personality.

Black Bridge

Running through the graveyard was a busy train line spanned by the Black Bridge and the White Bridge. The parapet of the White Bridge formed a big high curve over which I once crawled for a dare. I wouldn't recommend it. I was shaking for half an hour after. Next to the Black Bridge was a hole in the fence where we could crawl through and place coins on the track.

They would leave an imprint of Britannia or King George on the track but the coin itself, flattened and sharp edged, would shoot off and have to be searched for. My pride and joy was a ha'penny run over by the Golden Arrow. Yes folks, a real steam train.

(May I emphasise for the benefit of my younger readers that playing around on a railway track is extremely dangerous and totally illegal. I didn't do it really. I have included this bit of fiction just to add a little drama to my otherwise true biography.)

Beyond the graveyard was the River Don, which always held a fascination for us kids. In the period before bonfire day, (by which I mean any time after July) we would drag logs, tyres or branches out of the river and struggle sometimes for hours up the steep hillside and down Teynham Road to our back garden.

Usually we would put wellies on if we went to the river but invariably we would go too deep and get a welly full of brown, foul sulphurous ochre water. (The unit for measurement of depth in the Don at that time was the British Standard Welly.)

Near to the river bridge at Club Mill Road was a tributary which ran from just below the Five Arches railway bridge on Herries Road and under what is now Cooper's Scrap yard. The stream came out of a tunnel known as "Smitten Entry".

Presumably the name was due to sewage outflows entering the stream but nevertheless it was cleaner than the river itself and a small colony of tiddlers and sticklebacks survived if they didn't swim too far into the chemistry lesson called the River Don.

(It wasn't really called Smitten Entry but it has occurred to me that with a little care this book could be a valuable historical document for younger readers as well as adults. I have therefore removed the real name which was not Smitten Entry at all, though it did include the word "Entry.")

'Smitten' Entry near Five Arches Bridge,
as it is today, now with a grid preventing access
and serving as a sophisticated filter

Me and Gus would wade in and catch little fish with our bare hands, which we took home in a rusty tin can to transfer into an old enamel bucket.

On one occasion we took loads of fish home and when a few had died because we had no idea what to do next with them, we decided to take the whole bucketful back to the river.

Half way down the Medders our Gyp decided to do his run-at-your-legs routine and I was knocked flying. We were reduced to hurriedly scrabbling about in panic on the clay track, scooping up anything with signs of life back into the bucket which by now contained about half a cupful of water-just about enough to keep the bellies of the fish damp.

We then ran like hell over the White Bridge, through the zig-zag maze, through the cemetery and down to the river where we unceremoniously dumped the fish just as they were taking their last breath or drink or what ever it is they do.

Not all of my leisure time was spent on constructive pursuits like murdering fish. Me and Gus once spent a whole half term teaching swear words to the kid next door but one. We got in big trouble over that. Sometimes in the boring rainy days between school terms we had to find meaningful ways of passing the time.

I recall one day when me and Gus decided to come down our stairs in as many ways as we could imagine.

These included the following:-

Without touching the stairs. On head and hands only. On a sledge. On a bike. On a bike made from a tandem. Both on the same bike. On bum, no feet allowed to touch, carrying a dog. Sledging on a stepladder. Doing most of the above dressed as my dad.
Doing most of the above dressed as my mam.

And kids today say they have nothing to do!

Five Arches Bridge. Gateway to Sheffield 5 and host to slogans such as Cut the Call Up or Fight Tory Rent Act

We made the best of the situation and divided the time available between the three most exciting of pastimes, namely menacing, prowling and scrounging.

Just when I had dressed myself up for that final stunt a meter reader or some such official came to the door and was met by an apparition which confused him somewhat. Half way through asking "Is your mam in" he realised the irony of his question, gave up and shambled away mumbling, presumably to put in for early retirement there and then.

During dark autumn evenings there was a strange magic in the air which seemed almost hormonal and all young lads got into mischief.

Our time was often restricted because Gus's mam always wanted him in early. Rather than admit this he made some excuse about not wanting to miss Dick Barton-Special Agent on the wireless.

We made the best of the situation and divided the time available between the three most exciting of pastimes, namely menacing, prowling and scrounging.

Scrounging was the name we used when we were actively seeking a den. We would tentatively examine disused chicken sheds, garden huts and secluded corners of other people's property in the unrealistic belief that we could make our own den there. That old song springs to mind.

'There ain't nobody here but us chickens'.

Prowling was the art of patrolling the estate on private property without detection. The excitement and the danger of getting caught was a thrill never to be forgotten.

On one occasion a woman came out and just stood there for ages at the back door just as we had entered her garden from next door. We dropped flat to the ground behind her comfrey, so close to her that we could hear her breathe.

However she didn't hear us breathe because we daren't breathe at all until she had lit a fag, smoked it down to nothing and gone back inside. When we eventually got up blue in the face and returned to the street lights we realised that we had been laid in a pile of soot which had been dumped on the garden.

Another trick was to stretch cotton across Donovan Road between two door knockers. We would then either knock on one door, two doors or just wait for the Hundred and Ten bus to come past and break the cotton.

Why did every householder and chimney sweep on our estate believe that a mixture of carbon and sulphur was good for the garden? Nothing ever grew where the soot was spread and all it did was make such a mess of a prowler's bath water that nobody wanted to follow you in. Menacing consisted of various mischievous acts such as running up the street throwing iris pods at windows then watching from a hidden spot whilst all the neighbours came out and muttered to each other.

(Now don't start getting on your high horse, you have all done it).

Another trick was to stretch cotton across Donovan Road between two door knockers.

We would then either knock on one door, two doors or just wait for the Hundred and Ten bus to come past and break the cotton. Householders at opposite sides of the street would come out, look up and down the deserted street and scratch their heads in puzzlement whilst we stood behind the privet stifling our laughter.

(I can just imagine some ninety year old bloke on Donovan Road, reading this and thinking "Ah so it was you was it, you little sod!)

Another of our pastimes was scrumping but unfortunately apple trees were not exactly numerous on our estate.

We had to go as far as the mental home at Grenoside and for obvious reasons this was surrounded by a high wall which was a bit of a challenge. We then found another supply of apples at Bishopsholme in Roe Woods. On the first attempt we were just reaching for the apples when a maid dressed in a proper maid uniform came out to shake a table cloth at the back door.

On seeing us she yelled "Let the dogs out George!"

We departed like a hare at Owlerton dog track and didn't stop running until we were in our own back yard, where we had actually been all the time, honest.

The other day I was chatting to my old Aunty and she told me that she had worked at the Bishopsholme herself at that time. The Bishops had long gone, thus reducing the number of Christians in Sheffield 5 by fifty per cent. The place had become a home for wayward girls, which might have suited the bishops quite well if they had still been there. They could have saved their souls. Aunty was able to confirm that there was indeed a man called George working there, but apparently our fears were unnecessary. There were no dogs!

Another pastime on fine summer evenings, was similar to scrumping but could be carried out without straying from our own "causey edge."

It is best explained in yet another of my world famous poems.

Here it is at no extra cost.

Batchelor's Peas

*Sheffield town in days gone by was
not only famous for steel
It had a factory known world wide,
with inner man appeal
In Beeley Wood by the River Don
among the waving trees
Was a thriving little industry – the
home of Batchelor's Peas*

*Procedure back in those days was
to pull the plants complete
Then heap 'em on a lorry and cart
'em down our street
O'er bumpy roads on breezy days
the odd bits went astray
And fell down from the lorry, and in
our gutter lay*

*Now loose loads aren't permissible
and littering's a sin*

*Street cleaning was essential, and
that's where we came in*

*We'd gather in the pea plants and
have a rare old time
An inner city harvest – suburban
feast sublime
(What a line eh!)
Even the pods were chewable, the
flavour was so sweet
Though the bits of inner lining we
spat out on the street
School dinner peas with bi-carb
were the worst peas you could get
But gutter peas were the freshest
peas. Even Batchelors hadn't got
'em yet*

*But on some summer evenings the
breezes didn't blow*

Get Thi Neck Weshed

Peas didn't grace the roadside and
we were full of woe
So we didn't think it evil, we didn't
think it wrong
With the aid of half a house brick we
kind of helped the peas along

Hid behind the police box in hopeful
mood we waited
With just the right trajectory and
angles calculated
(See, you get trigonometry and
physics all in with the price)
Then when the cab had passed us
by we'd pause for half a tick
And at the load of pea plants we'd
chuck the half a brick

Once more our good rich pickings
down in the gutter lay
I wonder if Dick Turpin had started
out this way

On very rare occasions, when in
anger and disdain
You find your tin half empty and you
write off to complain
It starts a chain reaction down at
Batchelor's peas
They want to sort the problem out-
they're very keen to please

They scrutinise their bunkers and
check out all their bins
They make sure that an extra pea
isn't in the other tins
They examine the conveyors and
check the weigh machine
But nowhere can the quantity of
missing peas be seen

But they don't know the secret.
They don't know the trick
They should look behind a police
box for a lad with half a brick!

If this less than conventional method of pea harvesting seems reckless
it should be seen in the context of the time, the traffic being much slower
and more scarce than today. However I make no excuses for the things
we got up to and I sometimes wonder how I managed not to go the way
of the aforementioned Patrick Rafferty, the phantom grave robber of old
Wardsend town.

So how did I cope with failing my scholarship? Firstly it should be
understood that nearly everyone failed, a bit like doing the pools.
Most of the kids just took it for granted that they would be going straight
up to the "Seniors" and their parents had little ambition for them.
For example, the Parent's Reply section on at least one of my reports
was filled in by our Norma.

Apparently when I was a baby my Mam went out of the room leaving me in the high chair but before she went she told Norma that under no circumstances must she press on my head, especially the soft spot in the middle.

It was uppermost in the minds of many parents that exam failure would mean their offspring would start earning one year earlier at the age of fifteen and would not require expenditure on bus fares or a school uniform. However my case was somewhat different.

My brother won something called a Birley Scholarship. Nobody quite knew what this was (and I still don't) but we knew it was only awarded to the top six in Sheffield. Alan went on to get a Physics degree. Norma passed her scholarship and later went to Oxford, a feat unheard of then in North Sheffield. In fact, regrettably it is not exactly common today. They both went to City Grammar and their conversations at home seemed so trendy and interesting that I would have liked to follow them, but it wasn't to be.

My mam and dad were not at all disappointed, in fact they never showed the slightest interest in our education and I suspect they were uncomfortable with the fact that their two eldest children seemed to be drifting into a different social and intellectual class.

Those parents of today who move house and job in order to live in the catchment area of a "Good School" would be consumed with envy if they could see Alan and Norma's educational success despite the total lack of interest which prevailed in our family and for that matter, our school, not to mention our neighbourhood.

But perhaps I am too hard on Shercliff School. It turns out that my failure to pass the Scholarship was due entirely to my sister, who recently confessed to me after a lifetime of guilt.

Apparently when I was a baby my mam went out of the room leaving me in the high chair but before she went she told Norma that under no circumstances must she press on my head, especially the soft spot in the middle, which of course she had no intention of doing until she was told not to.

2m/7/88/4724

CITY OF SHEFFIELD EDUCATION COMMITTEE

SHIRECLIFFE SECONDARY SCHOOL,

PENRITH ROAD,
SHEFFIELD, 5.

REPORT on the work of......*Graham Shepherd.*...... Form....*3A*.

for the School Year ended July, 19_59_.

SUBJECT	Maximum No. of Marks possible	MARKS EARNED	REPORT
	20	19	*Excellent. 1st in class.*
RELIGIOUS EDUCATION	10	8	
HANDWRITING	20	19	*Graham has the gift of putting down*
ENGLISH ESSAY	20	17½	*words in delightfully expressed*
" EXERCISES	20	20	*phrases & well-rounded, well-balanced*
" LITERATURE	20	19	*sentences. He should be a journalist even*
" SPELLING	10	10	*if only as a hobby. E.Wright*
" READING			
FRENCH	20	15	*Well done! Well deserved. A.V.*
GEOGRAPHY	20	18	
HISTORY			*Very good.*
CIVICS	20	15	*Has made good improvement.*
SCIENCE, GENERAL	80	54	*A very good result.*
MATHEMATICS, WRITTEN	20	17	*More care needed on the mechanical*
" MENTAL	20	13	*side.*
TECHNICAL DRAWING	20	13	*A steady worker who tries hard. H.*
NEEDLEWORK *METALWORK*	20	9	
MUSIC	20	10	
PHYSICAL EDUCATION			
OTHER WORK			
TOTAL	380	290½	

Position in Form 7 Number in Form 39. Number in Year /30

General Remarks *Graham is a very quiet, well behaved lad.*
He has tried extremely hard this year & his maths
particularly have improved. If he keeps up this effort
he should do extremely well. William A. Thomas. Form Teacher

Eric G. Robinson Headmaster

Parent's Remarks *We were glad to see the improvement in*
Graham's level in the class. The faults that
there are, have been constant throughout all his
reports and therefore do not seem to be because
of a lack of effort. We feel you have been very
successful in what you have made of him so far.
Do what you like in the future. You have our full
support. Mr & Mrs. Shepherd.

PLEASE RETURN TO SCHOOL

School report. Parent's remarks by sister
Norma but signed 'Mr. and Mrs. Shepherd.'

After a couple of years there was an opportunity to take an exam for Central Technical School

First she tried a little press which drew no reaction. She tried a bit harder. No reaction. Again even harder until this time I yelled and bawled my eyes out.

Norma gradually recovered from the shock over the next ten years until it was formally declared that I had failed my scholarship. She was in tears all that day at school believing that my failure was all her fault for pressing on my head when I was a baby.

So that is my excuse and I am sticking to it. Don't try it at home folks. The youngest and most precious members of your family could turn out like me.

So off I went to Shercliff Seniors. A few of the teachers there seemed a bit more interested in us and now that the top ten per cent had been creamed off to the Grammar Schools I was usually in the top levels in most subjects. Having been one of the smallest in the class all my life I went through a short-lived growth spurt which gave me a bit of confidence and I was quite a good runner for a while. I never quite got the knack of football and would avoid it when possible by playing Hockey or Rugby instead. At Rugby I could throw myself headlong at lads bigger than me and come out of it with their respect rather than a thick ear. (Actually I often did end up with a thick ear but inflicted in the interest of sport.)

All the pain was suffered in defence of our 'House' to which we had great loyalty and anyone whose misbehaviour led to a loss of house points was severely reproached by his house mates. On reflection the whole idea had merit, creating an element of group co-operation and utilising the aspect of peer pressure to shame a miscreant. The opinions of our peers were far more important than the canes wielded by our teachers.

After a couple of years there was an opportunity to take an exam for Central Technical School. Where was that? What was it? There was no preparation or information about what to expect, I was simply asked one morning if I wanted to take the exam.

I am still waiting to hear whether or not I have passed but I am not holding out much hope now. Anyway it's closed.

I remember these names by going through in my mind the old Colonel Bogie song

The senior school teachers were a mixed bunch. Some of them would be instantly forgettable if they had not been given such memorable nick names as Bullet Nooas, Vulture, Herman the German etc.

(I remember these names by going through in my mind the old Colonel Bogie song which relates their supposed physical shortcomings. "Bullet has only got one......." etc.)

There were two Mr. Thomasses, both Welsh and proud of it. They usually tried to see who could out-sing the other in assembly except when it came to their rendition of Guide Me O Thou Great Redeemer, especially the bit that goes,

"I will ever give to thee, (GIVE TO THEEEEE)"

At this point there was a rare moment of collaboration enough to make any red blooded Englishman want to emigrate to Wales and hug a miner.

Another character was Harry Altass. He was the metalwork teacher and I am guessing that he progressed to the job from a little mesters shop somewhere in Sheffield as he seemed to belong to the human race as opposed to the teacher genus.

His Christian name was sometimes permitted, he had a Yorkshire accent and he even let an odd swear word slip.

One day we were all gathered round him listening to detailed instructions on how to file a bar of metal, when Hobson, standing behind me, started getting on my nerves. I was wearing trousers cut down from some which had belonged to our lodger Dave and the needlecraft had not been a raging success.

Hobson kept whispering "baggy pants" in my ear and shaking the vast expanse of spare material which was flapping quite a distance from my backside. Harry Altass saw what was going on and after a while he quietly said to me,

"You can hit him if you like."

With that I whipped round and gave Hobson a real crack. I then said,

"Thank you sir."

Altass continued explaining as though nothing had happened.

But when Hobson stood up again he didn't mess about with my trousers any more.

Herman the German was the art teacher. I was rubbish at art and he was rubbish at teaching it, in fact he was just rubbish at any kind of communication. In fact he was just rubbish. His idea of teaching art was to let kids paint. That's all there was to it. What a job.

One day in the middle of a lesson and for no reason at all Herman just started staring at me with no expression on his face and it went on for absolutely ages and ages. I went red, yellow, green and white but he just stood there glaring whilst I felt like squirming into the nearest hole. Eventually he just went back to not teaching us anything as though nothing had happened.

To this very day I am totally puzzled as to what it was all about. And I still don't know if he was a real German because he didn't have an accent because he didn't speak. Enjoy eternity Herman. I'm sure there will be room down there for one more crap teacher.

There was one teacher at Senior School who shone above all others in terms of the inspiration she gave to her pupils, and I'm sure that many Old Shercliffians will agree. Miss Wright, otherwise known as Ena, was a pleasant, well rounded spinster who was not afraid to have a bit of a laugh in the classroom and created in every one of her charges a feeling of self worth. She commanded everyone's attention without needing a cane or a sharp tongue.

After many years of teaching English she never tired of correcting bad grammar or explaining the structure of a sentence. She was in love with her subject, and by the time she had finished with us, so were we. She wrote a few books herself. One was a children's story book which never got accepted by publishers. Another more successful one, called "The Art and Heartache of Teaching" was about herself, and about us!

On occasions the classroom discussions would drift miles away from the subject in hand, and Ena would treat us to some tale of her private life, which no other teacher would ever dream of doing.

In an autobiography we were studying, called Brother to the Ox, the author Fred Kitchen wrote several full chapters about meeting and falling in love with his wife, who died at a young age.

Old Gyp and Graham, having
progressed to long 'uns

But his second wife was acknowledged in the next chapter by the simple opening words, "I had married again by then..."
We discussed this at length and Miss Wright concluded that in her opinion there is only one real love in life for each of us. With that she stood there and wept openly in front of the class. During the war her fiancé had gone down in a submarine and never came back.

All in all most of the teachers did their best but with hindsight I can't help feeling that we were groomed for a working class existence in the Sheffield factories.

For every lad who learned about hack saws and how to file a bit of steel, somewhere else in the world people were learning about political history, the legal system, economics, how to do a CV or even how to pass the bloody scholarship. (Don't get me going again.)

When I was in the fourth year I was going round the school filling up ink wells and when I got to Miss Wright's room she said "Are you going to have a go at this RSA thing then?" I had no idea what she was on about but I thought she wanted me to take an exam which some older boys were doing, just for interest and I assumed it was to happen there and then that day, so I said I would have a go. It turned out that I would have to stay on for a whole year and do a special syllabus.

The RSA idea was gradually sold to me as an opportunity to catch up with my Grammar School contemporaries and obtain qualifications.

The advent of comprehensive education was soon to begin and the RSA exam was about to replace GCE nationally according to our Head Teacher. Well you can't be right all the time can you?

What really happened was that CSE came in instead at comprehensives as a forerunner of GCSE, and GCE at grammar Schools continued for quite a while, so RSA never took off. (Are you still with me?)

All the prospective employers and further education recruiting staff, on reading my CV, seemed to ask the same question – what the bloody hell is an RSA? And I was not well versed enough to answer them.

I had a certificate listing eight of them, including several distinctions, but nobody really explained what they were.

I knew it stood for Royal Society of Arts, but art was the only subject my course didn't include.

Why did an arts society set exams in maths, science and metalwork etc.? I didn't understand then and I don't understand now.

You may be aware that 'The Star' does a regular feature in which they interview a successful person and ask them, amongst other things, if they can remember the advice of their careers advisor and if it was of any benefit.

Without fail every answer to date has been a sarcastic negative. If you happen to be the head of Sheffield Council please would you get in touch? I have a simple proposal, how to cut the budget of the careers department to zero overnight with no loss of efficiency, thereby reducing my Council Tax bill from massive to just merely extortionate.

Anyway despite all that I managed to get a job on four pounds five shillings a week whereas the apprentices of the day were starting on two pounds fifteen and six. I was rich enough to trazz around on an old motor bike and fuel it up with half a crown's worth of four star every week.

I also drifted into the ever open arms of the further education system. All my classmates at Neet School had good GCEs and I soon learned that my RSA qualifications were no match for the completely alien syllabus I was presented with at Pond Street College, or its quaint but glorious outpost, Bowling Green Street Annexe.

I remember getting 4% in one exam when I had simply never been taught anything on the exam paper.

This incident reminds me of a story from my old English teacher Miss Wright. She once marked an exam paper on which, in desperation a hapless child had written

"God knows what this question is supposed to be about." She wrote in red at the bottom of the page, "God, ten out of ten, you none."

On one occasion at college I suddenly realised what the examiner wanted and I was writing furiously when the dreaded words came,

"Pens down please!"

In frustration I scribbled under the half finished work, that I had run out of time.

When the paper was handed back, underneath my statement "No more time!" in red ink were the words "No more marks!"

Well I deserved that one I suppose.

Despite the pitfalls I persevered with my further education for years and I quite enjoyed the social side, making many friends at day release and neet school, amongst the appreciators of motor bikes and under age drinking dens in the town centre.

Day release was in fashion at the time and looking back, perhaps I didn't know when to admit that my education was complete.

Now I probably have more letters after my name than my university educated brother and sister together, though it took many long years to get to that point and the letters I have are so obscure that I don't think I will ever get into Who's Who? Never mind. If one day someone publishes a more down to earth version simply called "Who???" then my name might appear.

Perhaps such a publication could be my next literary venture. I certainly know enough unheard-of people to fill a book and they are all remarkable and interesting if one is prepared to probe beneath the veneer. Actually most of them are Yorkshire tykes and don't have a veneer.

I maintain that intelligence must be hereditary because Degrees, MScs and PhDs abound among my three offspring and as their dad I claim full credit. Well that's my story and I am sticking to it.

Perhaps when children inherit their father's brain cells the mechanism is that the kids take his share. My gradual mental decline certainly makes it seems that way. Anyway I am very proud of my kids, though to me their personal qualities are far more important than academic achievements.

I was thinking of adding another picture to our wall amongst all the mortar boarded, certificate-waving young faces.

I recently found my old cycling proficiency certificate and wanted to frame it for our "Clever Wall" but when it came to a democratic decision my idea was massively out-voted by the wife.

No sense of humour some people.

All in all, life has been very good to me despite dubious beginnings and a mediocre early education. I may not have achieved anything remarkable but every day of my life is a pleasure and I am glad to be part of a close and happy family which is the envy of people who have had far more opportunities in life than I have.

And at least I have written a book.

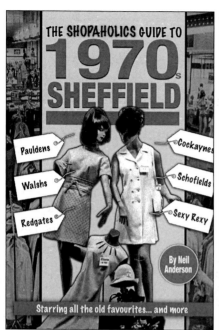

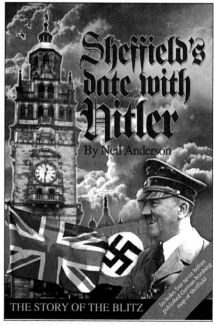

The Author

Graham Shepherd lived in the Parson Cross/Shirecliffe area from 1945 until 1970 when he married Hilary and moved to Deepcar.
He has three grown-up sons, all of which have settled with girls who are much loved additions to the Shepherd Clan. He has three grandchildren and hopes for more in time to come.
Graham spent all his working life in the ever-decreasing Refractories industry and has suffered redundancy on four occasions when he could least afford it.
In addition to writing poems and song lyrics, his interests in life have included vintage motor bikes, sailing and folk singing as well as voluntary youth work and involvement with the local Community Association.
He is currently local rep for South Yorkshire Badger Group which takes him out into remote corners of the great Yorkshire countryside as often as possible.

Dedication

I dedicate this book to my grandchildren. May they find joy and humour in their young lives and turn out like their parents.

Proofing: Peter Eales.
Proofing and balancing the books: Ian Cheetham
Book design and layout: Afb Creatives
Mail order: Karen Davies

A typical Parson Cross view

Hearing God

Beyond Grief

A Journal of Healing

KATHERINE DENISE BRYANT

Trilogy Christian Publishers
A Wholly Owned Subsidary of Trinity Broadcasting Network
2442 Michelle Drive
Tustin, CA 92780

10 9 8 7 6 5 4 3 2 1
Library of Congress Cataloging-in-Publication Data is available.
ISBN 979-8-89041-700-8
ISBN 979-8-89041-701-5 (e-book)

Dedication

Dedicated to all the grieving hearts who have lost loved ones, especially to my children, Nathan, Krista, Matthew, and Andrew, who lost their dad way too soon. To family and friends who never stop praying for me.

This is my story of my husband leaving the earth and entering heaven.

In August of 2020, my husband, Larry, became sick. We later found out it was COVID-19, which most of our family got and then recovered. But two weeks later, Larry ended up in the hospital, isolated from all of us, left to die… alone.

Even knowing what I know about who God is and what He has done for us on the cross, I was still having a hard time reaching Him during this grieving process.

Five weeks in, Jesus came to me in an awesome vision and gave me hope that I had misplaced since Larry had died, and I was so thankful for this. But still, my heart hurt, and I missed him so much.

I continued to do my devotions every day but did not have the confirmation of deep communication with the Father that I so longed for. Then, in November of 2021, I started a dialogue with God.

Two weeks later, a friend of mine gave me this book, *Joyful Journey: Listening to Immanuel,* as a gift, and it explained this new vein of communication I had found and opened up a journey I have been enjoying ever since.

This booklet/devotion is a compilation of the things I have heard as I sit quietly before the LORD and allow Him to continuously heal my heart through His presence. I pray these words to bless and touch you in a way that only He can. Thank you for allowing me to share this journey with you.

Me: Thank You, God, for this day.

LORD: Let me speak to you today.

Me: Please, LORD, do!

LORD: Lift up your eyes and see what I have done for you.

Me: LORD, show me!

LORD: See the results of the wind as it blows this way and that way, see how it moves the clouds in the blue sky, see the color of fall on the trees, see how those birds fly effortlessly. You know all of this I made for you to enjoy, for you to find peace in, for you to believe Me!

Me: LORD, I thank You for all these things, but my desire most is to be in Your presence and knowing I Am with that tangible knowledge.

LORD: Then look deeper, look beyond what you see. Open your spirit and look with the Holy Spirit into the things I have already put in front of you.

Me: Okay, okay, I see the squirrels climbing, moving, climbing higher; help me, LORD, to move this flesh and reach higher, go deeper in You. The birds fly, LORD, I want to soar in You! The trees are letting go of the old to make way for the new. Help me do this!

LORD: And in all this, the sun is shining, still rising and setting every day just like my Son is still shining on you, in you every day while you do the things you were meant to do. Go ahead, write it, "Girl, I got you." ox's

Me: Thank You. ox's

12/11/21

Thank You, God, for this day. Thank You, God, that I can put pen to the page, and You use it to write revelation to me, through me:

"I give you all that is before you,
I take away all that you will allow Me to.
I Am the giver of life,
I give you sustaining breath every second of
your life,

Though you have walked through the valley of the shadow of death,

I have been with you.
I never left you."

12/15/21

Thank You, God, for this day. See me farther along. You do see me this way. Give me sight to see.

"Give the light you have to give.
Shine in the places you are sent to.
Bring life that is inside of you to those dying
around you.
Live to the fullest. I have sat before you.
You and Me together are a force to
be reckoned with."
God speaks, I write. LORD,
always download to me!

12/17/21

I started reading the book today that explained what I had been doing as I communed with God. It gave me confirmation that I can hear Him.

Thank You, God, for this day. I hold my pen as a skilled writer, but it is not me who writes. Without the Holy Spirit, I have nothing to say that would credit to life in any way. I only want to write what You (God) cause to come to my mind!

> *"Keep your eyes focused and your senses keen.*
> *You can not go wrong when you trust in Me."*

LORD, there is a place we all want to get to, whether we know it or not. Sometimes, we feel like we are right there and just beyond the veil, the invisible realm. We could touch it, see it, feel it, and then…

No, but we must press in because I believe this is what You (God) want for us: to be in the moment, to see into the Spirit; all things You are doing in and around us. God, let me see!

Thank You, God, for this day and for healing for my family and body.

"These are the ways I have given you to stand, open your mouth, speak the truth, stand on My word, resist the enemy, and watch him flee. I Am all you need in all that comes; look to Me, hear Me, see Me, be in the moment with Me. You are mine, and I Am yours. We are going to defeat all and everything that would raise its head against you, your family (my family). *I Am your protector, your defender, your justice".*

12/19/21

Thank You, God, for this day and the insight that you have for me today. Here I am, LORD, fill me up.

"I pour through you like the oil that flowed through and into the vessels of the woman with her last meal planned. It will not run dry but will always be available as long as you are pouring out. See the vessels as people, the oil as my liquid love that you share with all you meet and live with, this love, this oil is life and anointing, joy and peace, change atmospheres, stay in My presence even when you are not up here (in my loft). I Am with you always."

12/20/21

Thank You, God, for this day, I enter into Your courts with praise and thanksgiving, for You are the giver of life, and I am grateful.

LORD: "Let this day bring glory and honor to Me. Let Me show you favor today."

Me: "How do I let You? How do I receive from You, to be the one who says, 'God, what do You want to do for me today?'"

LORD: "Just let it happen. I Am with you; never leave you, see Me around you, feel Me inside you. Give Me all your doubts, your uncertainties. I will make a way, always make a way for you. You are Mine, I take care of Mine, and when you have that thought, every time you hear this, even though you don't understand, I need you to know I took care of Larry, I was there, I never left him, and he is here, perfect!"

Me: "Thank You, God."

LORD: "You are precious to Me. Look for the surprise I have on this day for you!"

12/21/21

Thank you for this day, God. Sorry I don't have the time I would like to spend here, but You are with me every step of the way. Speak to me often and always.

> *"Before you start your day, always bow your head and pray. Focusing in on My light will make all your seasons bright. When you feel down about your loss, look up and remember what I did on the cross."*

12/23/21

Thank You, God, for this day.

"I Am your God, the God of your children, and the God of their children. We are there right now with you, with Nathan, his family, your whole family, and when we are present, nothing can stop you. Only believe, only receive what Jesus did on the cross, just for this, sickness and disease have to die in the light of My glory and grace, breathe in all of Me."

Thank You, God, for this day.

"Write this down and keep on writing, for life and liberty are in the writing of all who know the truth. I Am in the pen, I Am in the hand, the heart of the writer! I long to fulfill the desires of your heart and give to you all that I have for you. Rest in Me, be still in Me, and know the deep that you long for. You are mine, and I Am yours. We are one. We flow together. I have made it this way. Just as your hand writes what you are hearing, I can do this with your feet to go where I need you to. Your voice speaks what I need you to. You are blessed and highly favored."

Thank You, God, for speaking to me.

12/27/21

Thank You, God, for this day.

"Be in the moment, in everyone, and live to the fullness of every day. Cast your cares every day. Start afresh and anew because My mercies are new every morning. Stop trying to fix everything. Allow Me to do that. It is My job or My pleasure to do this for you. Give Me your sons and daughters, your grandchildren, and let Me take care of them and see their destiny unfold before you and them. Before you leave this room, see yourself taking the peace, the joy, that I have poured out on you and carry it with you this day."

12/28/21

Thank You, God, for this day.

"I love to talk with you. I Am sorry you have had a difficult time knowing that I have always been here, listening and answering you. I Am glad for the steps you are taking, seeking Me and getting closer to Me and all I have for you. I Am glad you found the little hints and clues along the way. I know you love that, like puzzle pieces, line upon line. Seeking out the treasure. I have so much in store for you. I can't wait for you to see it all, feel it all. Keep calm and carry on."

12/30/21

Thank You, God, for this day. Thank You for yesterday. Sorry that I just didn't feel focused enough to write, but I am here to listen, to write, to hear, to enjoy the pleasure of Your company.

> *"Be a voice. Let Me speak through you to those who are hurting, those who are disappointed. Don't let the past keep you from reaching out to all who need My touch, My love, My embrace. I have your back. I Am holding you up as you go."*

12/31/21

Thank You, God, for this day. I am so excited to read in these books and devotions the things I feel You are showing me in life. Let me use all these things to help others. Thank You for the peace that surpasses all things in You.

> *"If you find yourself in the desert, it doesn't matter how you got there, look for Me. I Am your water, your shade, your sustenance. I Am your deliverer. I never leave you or forsake you. No matter how hot or cold, I Am all you need in every situation. I will come for you, tangibly. I will lift you up out of those places because you are Mine. Let peace melt over you. Feel it, sense it, touch it, be in it. There will come a time in your life (cause I already have done it and see it) that nothing can touch you either emotionally or physically. Your spirit is intact. It knows these things. Rest in Me!"*

1/1/22

Thank You, God, for this day, for this New Year!

"Write for the widows,
Write for the orphans,
Write for the ones on the side of the road.
They are so heavy they carry so much; tell
them I Am here to lighten their load.
Show them the love that was poured out for
them.
Show them the freedom, the peace, the rest, all
that was done through Him!
Let them know I have given them My best!"

Thank You, God, for this day. Please speak and let me hear and see what You are calling me to.

"Your flesh wants to think this is cliché, but what does My word say? It is hearing and hearing that gets people's (your) attention. I Am all you need. I choose to bring favor to you and your family. I Am thrilled you would crave out time each day to sit with Me. Just listening to hear so you could write it down. This is not futile. This is life, the breath of life that will keep you and your destiny intact. The closer, the more you listen, the greater and more you will hear and, yes, feel in My presence."

1/3/22

Thank You, God, for this day. The snow is falling outside my window up here in this loft, then I come to be in Your tangible presence to hear from You and write it down. I thank You for this beautiful snow.

SNOW

Sins are washed as white as snow.
Just as snow covers dirt and decay.
I came, lived, and died to set you free.
I rose again that glorious day and gave new
light to show the way.

This book (*Joyful Journey*) talks about rhyming with You, God. I don't know if this is what it means yet, but this is what I have done, trying hard to hear. It shouldn't be a hard thing, and I don't want it to be. I just want to hear You, God.

Thank You, God, for this day. For bringing me higher, deeper, and reaching for more wisdom, and understanding.

"As the sun warms your face, let Me bring the scripture to you, 'The LORD bless you, the LORD make His face shine upon you' (Numbers 6:24). Realize that My face and My brightness are so much more than the sun. I can light the way when you think there is none. I Am the light in the darkness when you think, 'Where are You?' I Am always with you. I Am your beacon in all the waves that you think are overwhelming. Keep your eyes on Me. I will lead you, direct you, and always keep you."

1/5/22

Thank You, God, for this day. I am so blessed to hear from You. You are my everything.

"You know I ordain what you are excited about? Seek, and you shall find. You keep seeking, you will keep finding. It is the truth set in stone, not to change. I have great things for you, and we will find these together, you and Me, always together."

1/6/22

Thank You, God, for this day, for Your goodness and grace for moving in me and me sensing You and acting on that. Thank You for this precious child, Hayley, telling me Larry loves me and is proud of me.

"I know your thoughts on that and your feeling of not being sure if you can believe, but here's the thing, you already know that Larry loves you and is so proud of you. He told you this often, and I hope you know and believe that I Am proud of you and love you beyond anything. Thank you for sitting in your room and taking the time to write, listen to Me, and hear what is next in your life. If you listen and seek, you will hear Me, I hear you, and I Am here to answer. Now enjoy this day. My face shines on you."

1/7/22

Thank You, God, for this day.

"I do hear you. Thank you for trying to write down your thoughts and feelings. You can trust Me with them and be okay with whatever is there. You know the love and acceptance you showed Hayley. Where do you think that comes from? You are right, from years ago when you said in Exodus 32:7–14, 'where Moses talked to me about saving the lives of the people, that the passion he had as he felt compelled to intervene for them, came from me.' Don't doubt the gifts within you. You are Mine, you hear Me, you see Me!"

1/8/22

Thank You, God, for this day. LORD, I want to hear, see, know, and hunger for You more.

Song...

You are My sunshine
You let My Son shine
You make Me happy, all through the day
I always tell you, I hope you know it, you'll
never leave My Son shine to stray.

Thank You, God!

Thank You for this day. I will be glad and rejoice in it.

"Go, enjoy. I Am here,
and I will meet you there."

1/11/22

Thank You for this day, God.

> "As high as the mountains,
> as deep as the seas,
> My love for you is more than these!
> What you know and what you don't know
> doesn't keep you from what I have prepared for
> you in this time, this season, this hour of your
> life. I will guide you, train you, lead you into all
> I have for you. You are a treasure to Me, always
> have been,
> always will be."

1/12/22

Thank You, God, for this day.

"What is a legacy of love? What does it look like, where will it take you, who will it touch? I say it will touch all you see, all who come in contact with you. And you think that it's just about a man, a love, that you once had, but now is gone, but I say look much higher and deeper to a love that never leaves you, that would pour itself out for you on a cross and go to the farthest ends of everything just to be with you. Now, that is what a legacy of love really is.
I AM LOVE!"

1/13/22

Thank You for this day, God.

"Yea though you walk through the valley of the shadow of death, you will fear no evil, for I Am with you. You have done this and continue to do this, and you are getting a hold of I Am with you. I never left LB or BK, and they are perfect in My sight. Keep seeking, keep walking, and keep on with no fear. I Am here, and I will lead you. You will find the mysteries you are searching for. Just as you enjoy your children finding or opening secrets you have planted for them, so do I. I Am so thrilled to have you follow after Me and find the clues I have left you. And I have left them all along your journey. Enjoy finding them."

1/14/22

Thank You, God, for this day.

> "Bring life into every situation; that is what
> I have called you to. Let Joy arise within you
> because it's there for you when you need it,
> each and every time. I Am with you always,
> never to leave."

1/15/22

Thank You, God, for this day.

"As the sun shines on your face, look up and know I Am shining on you. Know the warmth and peace in the light of My face. I see you and know you. Love the bright warmth of My love. I Am here for you no matter what you see, hear, or go through.
I Am here. I will always be here in every moment of every day. Leading you and telling you which way to go, seek out that which I have put in your path for you to find. Enjoy this journey you are on, and I will show you great things in the midst of this world of darkness. Follow the light, live in the light, be the light."

Thank You, God, for this day.

I had a thought earlier that I wanted to share with You, and now, as I sit here to write it, I can't think of it. Maybe that is a good thing. Sometimes, deep thoughts are better to be forgotten. I pray You know anyway and take care of them.

> *"Don't let the lies of the enemy control who you are. Feelings are not you. Let the Holy Spirit blow these feelings, these lies, off and away from you, just like the wind is blowing this snow around. You are white as this snow Jesus has covered you completely, and I see His righteousness all over you. You are transforming daily as you sit in My presence. I long to be with you, to have your graze, your attention, to put puzzle pieces into place together. I enjoy the seek and find, like you do. Let's seek out this word; 'Hippocratic oath is rooted in mythology.'"*

I didn't know this, don't know why I thought of this word today, hoping You showed it to me.

Confirm to me, God, what you are showing me? The oath's original form requires a new physician to swear by a number of "healing gods."

1/18/22

"So many things are trying to bid for your mind space. I see you being on the edge of worry or concern in your life and your business, but if you remember, I have told you over and over I will show favor to you and the business and your family. Trust Me, that word that you all want so much to be true of your earthly vessels. Keep feeding it with My words, keep listening to Me and writing it all down. I will show you things you have longed for, and we, together, will walk out your destiny. You are a light in this dark world, and you do shine. I have made you that way, and I have so enjoyed watching you grow and become more and more like Me. Fear not. Take courage, 'the best is yet to come!'"

1/19/22

Thank You, God, for this day.

"You have heard as the deer panteth for the water so my soul longeth after You. You alone are my heart's desire, and I long to hear from You. Your spirit yields to Me; don't try so hard to make this happen. It's not up to you to cause it. I Am ready to speak with you and commune with you. My desire is to bless you and bring joy into your life. Believe Me and trust Me as you are doing, and let Me show you the marvelous future ahead of you. Thank you for your giving heart and willingness to listen and love well. I've got you!"

Thank You, God, for this day. The red birds came again this morning. Thank You for that. The beauty of Your nature thrills me, how You created everything for me, for us to enjoy, to be in awe of.

> *"Lift up your voice, cry out to Me all the things you want to cry out. I Am here for that. Walk beyond the mundane to a place I have for you. Let your spirit rest in that place and make your flesh-hungry for it. You will succeed in all your ambitions. You will do what few men have done before."*

1/21/22

Thank You, God, for this day. For my life and my family, for friends and people who need Your love and power of healing, let me pray and speak their names and cover them with the name of Jesus. I need to move my body, to get up and live. I need to have the desire to function in this world and ministry.

> *"As the olive tree blooms in the desert, so you*
> *will bloom in the place I have you planted. As*
> *the trees are by the water, so are you being*
> *nourished by Me and what I Am bringing you.*
> *You are a joy to me. You shine bright for Me.*
> *I look at you and see My Son. You sometimes*
> *doubt all you are and what I want to do in you,*
> *but you don't need to. I will accomplish what*
> *I have for you; don't ever let go of that dream,*
> *that knowing inside you. If only for a moment*
> *you can see it, it will come to pass, and you will*
> *have joy so much joy. You will spread it around*
> *just like you were created to do. I love My time*
> *with you!"*

1/22/22

Thank You, God, for this day. And the answers that you bring my way. To prayers, to request, to just live this life, to help others, and to be a light for all to see.

> *"Let the well of My presence spring forth from the very depths of you. Watering all around you. Let the fruit of My labor, not yours, grow in you and flourish. You are required to believe and trust. Believe My glory surrounds you. Trust My presence that's in you. Let's turn this world upside down and right side up to fulfill the word I gave to men. Stay close to My presence."*

Thank You, God, for this day. For my child, like faith, for that is how I want to be, to trust You completely with everything.

> *"I have called you to walk on the mountain tops. You are not prone to the valleys. That is because you were created for the mountain tops, to run and jump from mountain to mountain, or glory to glory. You can see much farther on the top of a mountain than what's in front of you. You can hear much clearer on top of the mountain. There are no shadows on the mountaintop. Come up higher."*

Thank You, God, for this day.

I think. I wrote a few days ago about how I had stopped counting the months after the year mark, but this month of the New Year, I realized that the day was close, and I was not affected as I was the first year, but just noticed and counted up the months—sixteen months since Larry passed and came to heaven with You God. For the whys, I don't know, but I do know that because of You, I am whole than I was four months ago. My heart is guarded by You.

> *"Breathe in and breathe out. This is the rhythm of life. Life in Me is a symphony of beautiful music of us moving together as we/you journey through this land on the earth, and one day, when the high notes are played, the climate will be so great you will be rewarded just for saying yes, and participating in this great orchestra. I Am the conductor, and you are a masterful musician that I lead, and you follow."*

Thank You, God!

Thank You, God, for this day. For the encounters I will have today. Let my/Your light shine in me and around me.

> *"Trees are strong, and the deeper the roots, the stronger they are, and they do not toil. They just do what they do: stand tall in the soil. The wind blows, and they may sway, but if the roots are deep, it matters not what comes, wind, rain, snow, or hail. If your roots/ foundation is deep in Me, you will stand tall. Just do what a child of Mine would do, stand and be who you are created to be and let the fruit multiply."*

1/26/22

Thank You, God, for this day.

"Always look to Me for life, and love is in Me. I Am your anchor in a sea of doubt and raging circumstances. Hold, live, and know I Am with you every step of the way to defeat the enemy. You shine and stay close. I have given you all you would ever need to take on this task of standing and proclaiming truth and life over you and your family. Burn the enemy down with your praise and worship of Me. I Am all you need. I Am the deliverer in every scenario that comes your way. Breathe and rest. Peace prevails in your life, your body. I Am here! Right here with you!"

1/27/22

Thank You, God, for this day. What do you want to say to me today, God?

> *"There is a view from where I sit (and you are*
> *sitting here too(that makes everything clear*
> *at the moment you need it and will always be*
> *your lifeline in times when there seem to be no*
> *answers or a way to be on top of whatever it is.*
> *I Am here, I see the plan and the future, and it*
> *is so good. I want you to see, to open your eyes,*
> *because you are right here beside me. We are*
> *seated together. Believe and breathe and live*
> *to the fullest. The enemy is Our/your footstool;*
> *make him your footstool. I made the way for*
> *you too."*

Song...

There's a well down in my soul and its deeper
still you know,
And it springs up with the life you've given me,
Let it flow from deep within, where you are and

where you've been,
Bringing waters to the dry and thirsty souls'
who are crying from their sin,
To a place they've never been, let the water
bring life to make them whole.
It can only come from You, God, creator of this
well that's in my soul.

1/28/22

Thank You, God, for this day.

> *"Pour the oil of joy on everyone today. Pour it on yourself and be a joy for others as I Am your joy. Let My joy fill you to overflow and stay in it every moment of the day. Catch the words, the encounter that I have set for you this day. I will not disappoint.*
> *I can not."*

1/29/22

Thank You, God, for this day. And the joy You have put in it, in my soul and body. What does worship in Spirit look like?

"Everything you do is worship, but the best worship is to Me, spending time with Me, sitting in My presence and enjoying it. Worship in Spirit is when your heart is so in love with Me that you may not be doing anything with your flesh (bowing, kneeling, hands up), just being in the moment. Being still, but your heart is all in. Exploding with the passion of love that is worship in Spirit. Laying your life down, your time for someone else, that is worship in Spirit. Holding someone in their very hour of need, when they need that hug, that love, that is worship in Spirit."

1/30/22

Thank You, God, for this day. Open up Spirit to me to hear so clearly.

"Do not fear that I won't talk to you. That is the enemy of your soul. I enjoy talking to you. It brings Me pleasure that you would sit and listen. I can work with that to bring about what I have planned. You will accomplish what I have put in you to do. Not only that but you will be amazed and enjoy it. Keep leaning on Me, keep believing, trusting, walking, like Jesus, and you will see the salvation of your God (Me)."

1/31/22

Thank You, God, for this day, for closer and deeper conversation with You. Let me always bring worship and praise to You and know You in joy and find pleasure in it. God, I want to rest in You, in all things. My life, my business, my family, church, friends, and ministry, in what you have for me. To trust You completely in the face of anything, to be at peace and confident that You are there always, working all out for my good and Your glory. Help me get rid of the thoughts that You have used up all the words for me, and I can't write any more from You.

> *"Remember in My word, where it says, if all the things that Jesus did were written down, there would not be enough books to hold it all. Well, where do you think He got that? I will never run out of words for you. I could tell you things every moment of the day because that's how precious and important you are to Me. Do not let your heart be troubled. Trust Me always in all things."*

2/1/22

Thank You, God, for this day. For your goodness and love for me, give me your voice, your thoughts.

God, if I don't feel like I can hear your thoughts, do I press on and try to find words to write? Or do I just be okay? You are with me, You never forsake me. Let me rest in You and not be discouraged in any way, shape or form. For You are my creator. I live for You always. I breathe in You and find You there. I am seated in the heavens with You.

"Yes, you are!"

2/2/22

Thank You for this day, God. I loved writing that date. I pray for Sean F. today in all he is doing in Your Name, and bless him all day with twos. Favor on Your children today and every day.

> *"Take no thought in what you will say when you stand before men/women because you have the Spirit that knows all inside you, to lead and guide and say what needs to be said. Just do what you do best in this life, love with My love, look like Jesus, and the rest will fall in place. You know it is that easy and not a hard thing to lean on Me and trust Me!"*

"Yoke easy, burden light" (Matthew 11:28–30).

Thank You, God, for this day. For life and freedom, peace and joy. Speak, LORD, so I can hear.

"Trust and peace, you can't go wrong if you trust Me and follow peace. I Am the peace that has broken down every wall. Give peace, live in peace, rest in peace, let peace consume you and those around you. Carry peace. I told you a long time ago that you are a peacemaker."

Thank You, God, for this day. For Your goodness and grace that you have given me to live and function in this world. Let me continue to look like Jesus in all and every situation.

"A picture is worth a thousand words, so they say. A girl (you) on the mountainside in a vast meadow, arms outstretched. The space is huge, the air is clean, the sky is blue, and the view is grand. You can't see with your flesh eye, but I fill all that space around you. Every inch, every molecule. I want you to rest in this vision. I Am here, I Am with you."

Thank You, God, for this day. Open up the sky and pour down Your blessings, and know I want You more. I seek You for You, to know You, to follow You, and to hear Your voice always.

2/10/22

Thank You, God, for this day. For Your goodness to me, for Your presence right here in me, around me.

"Everything you put your hand to, I will prosper. I Am here. What do you want to do? Set your hand to it and see it come to pass. Live in Me, love in Me. Be all I have for you to be. It's okay to get excited about what is coming. Keep dreaming, keep moving in Me, for Me."

2/11/22

Thank You, God, for this day. For Your presence, for allowing me to kiss Your feet. Thank You for healing, for Your love picture of Jesus on the cross, that you love me sooooo much. God, you are precious, and You're glorious, beautiful, and marvelous.

> *"Take that, live it, that's where you go, where you walk, you carry My glory, the healing power of Holy Ghost, to do and be in My good pleasure. Walk, and your shadow brings wholeness. It's a real thing. Just let it happen. You can't help what flows out of you if you can only believe. I consume you, and I do dream big, live big. Trust BIGGER!"*

2/12/22

Thank You, God, for this day. God, I want to live in Your presence, this presence, this compassion always, every day, and touch lives so that they could feel this great love of the Father.

> *"I enjoyed the time you have spent with Me*
> *today, and you do not have to give up the*
> *presence when you leave this upper room. I Am*
> *with you, carry the glory with you to all you*
> *see, spread joy, love, peace, calm. Thank you*
> *for being available*
> *to flow through."*

Thank You, God, for this day.

"I have missed you and that believing heart of yours that melts when you 'get it!' You hear My words, feel My love, and I know you have missed Me too. Don't let things get in our way. Let nothing come between us. Your worship is precious, glorious, beautiful, and marvelous."

2/14/22

Thank You, God, for this day. Your day, God.

"Embrace this day with the love I have for you and put in your heart, to love others, to show what a love God I Am. A love that is everlasting and never leaves. I will never leave you. I Am the lover of your soul. Dance with Me!"

2/15/22

Thank You, God, for this day. For success in You in everything we set our hands to. Thank You for favor.

"I got you, just be willing to speak, to give out what I Am putting in you, and it will be an encounter that will match no other. They need to see the love, feel the love the way you are seeing it, feeling it. Just tell your story for Me."

2/16/22

Thank You, God, for this day. God, I want those moments where You know that You know. That You are in it "if not for God," only You, God, could do this. Bring that, be that, right here in the moment.

2/18/22

Thank You, God, for this day.

*"Lean into that feeling, that glory I put in you
to carry, to share. Encounters unlimited, every
day and everywhere. Live in every second,
know I Am there in those seconds and moments
of every day. I don't sleep or slumber or forget
you. I don't walk away, not for a moment. See
Me, hear Me, let Me come and do something for
you!"*

2/19/22

Thank You, God, for this day. God. I pray that all I say blesses and not hinders everyone. I don't want feelings and thoughts that are not You. God. I don't want to assume anything but just hear You. Check my heart, bring me fully alive to the gospel, fully alive in You and what I am to be and do. Wash from me, judgment, and any hindrance to and for another person that might try to rise in me.

2/20/22

Thank You, God, for this day.

> *"Let Me handle today and every day from here*
> *forward. Relax, rest, enjoy*
> *Me in this day."*

God, am I the reason You sing?

2/21/22

Thank You, God, for this day.

*" If you feel more confident in the clothes you
wear, if they are more up to date or classy or
however you think about them, but more with
an air of belonging or rightness, if you look
good, you feel good attitude. What you could
accomplish when you see yourself as you really
are with My robe of righteousness, My mantle,
My clothing, I cover you with. Walk with your
head up and let your flesh feel. I Am your
Father. You are Mine. Live, feel, breathe in this
knowledge."*

2/22/22

Thank You, God, for this day. God, I love all the twos in this date. I am ready to receive anything and everything You have for me at this time, when the time is ready. I know that time is not that important to You, or at least, I don't think it is. Maybe it is. Maybe this day does hold keys to doors, to open, to close. I pray with all Your people that it is what You have ordained it to be. Bless Sean F. today as he worships before the world and glorifies Your name. LORD, I to be led by You, feel Your presence, sense your anointing, to touch with Your touch.

"Follow My lead. I Am always there with you to help."

Prophetic word from a dear friend, M.W. God saying...

"I knew when I called you, it would be a struggle, but My goodness was factored in." This awful thing that happened (my husband's passing) is a blurb of time and can't touch the overall thing that He is doing.

Another lady said, "You wanted to gift me a love gift. An angel is bringing it."

LORD, I receive every and all gifts You have for me.

2/23/22

Thank You, God, for this day.

"Thank you for sharing your heart with these daughters yesterday. For allowing Me to touch them through you. For being willing to open your mouth and let Me fill it. And let the grace I have poured on you flow on to others. I know you wonder about My vessels telling you I Am proud of you, but I Am, so I will continue to say it, till you are comfortable with it, and then say it some more."

2/24/22

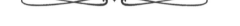

Thank You, God, for this day. For protection going to the beach, let this trip be just what You want it to be, LORD.

"Let Me do more than you can ask, dream, or imagine. I want to; don't hold back in worship or anything. I speak into you to do. Step beyond."

2/25/22

Thank You, God, for this day.

"You are banking up, putting in the time and, accumulating for others, that you care for."
Shine, LORD, shine, there is none like You, God none.

2/26/22

Thank You, God, for this day. God, I want to rest in You. Sleep, dream, and live in You. Think in You, speak, touch, and breathe in You.

3/4/22

Thank You, God, for this day. For Your goodness and revelation to me, more and more, on and on and on, today, of all that You are, I am.

"I Am your hiding place, I Am your peace and rest. I see you in this place. I love your longing for Me. I Am there, I have the angels you so desire to stand ready and guide you and your family, always with you. Seek and grow and learn all you can. I help you take in more than you could imagine. Thank you for hearing and putting help aids into the hands of My precious ones. Thank you for always choosing the best path, even when it is hard for you. You will be rewarded and satisfied, I promise."

3/5/22

Thank You, God, for this day. God, I don't want to get hung up on the past and think about what others have said or done to me. I am sorry if I talk too much about past hurts or offenses. I want to live in the now, this moment, and bless all people, past and present. I want to walk in the gifts You pour out and see the things You want me to.

> *"You are right to speak these things out. Don't hold back. It is My word, remember, it doesn't return void, but it does what I mean it, sent it, to do. Be bold, speak with confidence. I have your back, I've got you, I will see to it. Signs follow those that believe, Believe!"*

3/6/22

Thank You, God, for this day.

"Just be, and I will do the rest. When people cry out for more, more comes. Look for it, wait for it, touch it, reach out, and grab hold of the glory and the anointing."

3/7/22

Thank You, God, for this day. For wisdom and the way to do the things You give me to do.

Remember to take communion every day for forty days to rescue the babies.

May 14, big meeting concerning Roe vs. Wade. Dare to believe.

Rip veil over the nations.

3/9/22

Thank You, God, for this day.

> *"Angels sing around the throne,*
> *Angels soon will bring you home,*
> *I did it before, I will do it again,*
> *With your whole life on Me depend."*

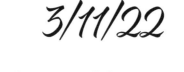

Thank You, God, for this day. Thank You for the fire. Baptize me all new and fresh with fire and love. Holy Spirit, baptize me again, over and over. Today, I went to a friend's house to pray, and one of the ladies sang over me from God. Something like this…

"I can see in your eyes, I see your face in the sun, new beginnings, and He sees me. I see your love, but more than that, I see your heart."

She said she was sensing His appreciation for my deep intimacy with Him.

3/13/22

Thank You, God, for this day. For the journey I am on to see. I look forward to the things we will do and what You will show me. Holy Spirit, how many angels are in this room? Are there three angels? My angel, Larry's angel, and my daddy's? Do their angels stay with me since they went to heaven?

"There are a hundred angels at any moment you need."

Thank You, God, for this day. God, help me with the feelings of my flesh, with dreams and things concerning it. I miss Larry, my body misses him too. I know who I am in You. I know this will pass. Hold me, God, comfort me. Focus and breathe; peace comes! God, You are faithful, and Your promises are true!

3/15/22

Thank You, God, for this day. God, speak to me in ways I can see, hear, feel, know that You see me. I feel I need Your reassurance every day. I know I live with You every moment. Why am I so needy of You? I want Your tangible presence with me always.

> *"You have it, open up your eyes and see. Just like the servant saw the army of the LORD. They are there surrounding you, protecting what is Mine. Just as you would tell others what I Am saying in the moment, the wind blowing, the birds singing, the sunrise, sunset, the blooms of the spring, let Me speak to you in all these things, and you will see. You are never without Me."*

3/16/22

Thank You, God, for this day. I think I am on the right path in all the books today. Purpose is the keyword, and yesterday, I started out seeing You in everything. Help me to do this even more, LORD, today and always.

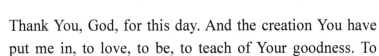

Thank You, God, for this day. And the creation You have put me in, to love, to be, to teach of Your goodness. To fulfill the purpose You have patented for me.

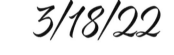

Thank You, God, for this day, for Your grace to see past the pain and hurt of life. To see the beauty and perfection You are in us, and all around us, with us, always.

"Be the piece of the puzzle, the solution in the moment, the anointing when needed. Moving in the Spirit, being and following My lead, that is life in Me. Love it, enjoy it, live it. I Am speaking; you are hearing!"

Thank You, God, for this day. Open up my chest and breathe on my heart.

3/21/22

Thank You, God, for this day. Let me please You. Peace and goodness on my soul always, LORD.

3/22/22

Thank You, God, for this day.

*"More than you can ask, dream or imagine.
I will be for you, be all this and more. Rest in
this, trust Me with it all."*

3/23/22

Thank You, God, for this day.

> *"My soul sings for you also. My deep calls to your deep. You hear Me. You can rest in Me. Seek and find and share with others. That's it, that's the life I have for you, keep it going, I Am here!"*

3/24/22

Thank You, God, for this day. Thank You for the knowledge to believe it is Your will to heal every time and that healing is always available.

"Green means life, means healing, means growth. Green is the color you see in your dreams. Why green?"

Thank You, God, for this day. For Your revelation of love, Your love, and the help and love You put in me to love well. I ask that it will grow bigger and greater each day, and I look like You, Jesus. Thank You, Holy Spirit, for always leading me into truth and grace to see, hear, and do the will of my Father.

> *"The thankfulness and praise for the goodness in you will only grow and be more and more as the time on earth goes by. It is okay for you to feel good because I work in you, and your prayer is granted that you look like My Son. You know this. Don't let anything stand in your way, My way of you shining even brighter and brighter. I love to shine through you, and others see this and the love you so graciously pour out."*

Thank You, God, for Your goodness and clear truth to me this day.

*"Denise, darling, you don't understand, but
you will, because you have decided to sit
and hear My words to you. I will open up the
understanding for you to receive all and know
all I want you to. I see you are devoted to Me, to
hear, to love, to speak. I will reward and bless
because I so want to make you happy and at
peace and rest in this life here and now. You
have found
favor with Me."*

3/29/22

Thank You, God, for this day. Thank You for joy and peace in our trust in You. And favor on our life, every part of it. God, I don't want to put You in a box of how I think things should be, but LORD, I have a relationship with You, and I don't want to go back into a box of condemnation and oppression in any way.

"Remember, always I see your heart, a pure heart, and your focus on Me. You won't be deceived in either ditch. You hear My voice and follow Me. I will lead you. The expectation of finding something new and exciting each day. I feel that, too, about you discovering new things or the things you see in a new way, with the glory highlighting it. The more you seek, the more you will find, I promise."

3/30/22

Thank You, God, for this day. Who told you, you couldn't see God's face?

Thank You, God, for this day, for speaking to me and me hearing Your voice and blessing Your children.

Thank You, God, for this day. For bringing me into peace, Your peace and goodness. Changing my atmosphere to Yours, knowing You have me, my family, my business. Making all things right in everything we put our hands to. We will see the favor of our God!

4/3/22

Thank You, God, for this day. Open my heart and soul to know you more.

> *"Your Father serves you food every day, eat and be filled with all you need. I withhold nothing from you. Gather that which is in front of you. Grow in the light of My love, and let the power and grace flow out of the inner most part of you. You are one blessed girl, My girl!"*

Thank You, God, for this day. Thank You for knowing me. The new aspect of You, I see this day. It is a great and powerful thing to see You and all You are more and more each and every day. I want to experience more.

4/5/22

Thank You, God, for this day. For Your goodness in me and the work You are doing. I want to write what comes to my mind, praying I hear from You always. Today the thought came that my man lost his earthly body, and I will see thousands raised up. The seeds he planted will rise, and God will reward and water and bring an increase in my lifetime. Thank You, Father God.

Thank You, God, for this day. Thank you for the word "magical," meaning beautiful and delightful in such a way as to seem removed from everyday life. Sounds like heaven to me. Living each day in You, God.

Word of the day—"mystical": inspiring a sense of spiritual mystery, awe, and fascination; a journey You have me on.

What a ride if we open our eyes to see what is really going on here, there, everywhere.

> *"Way back when you were a little girl, when the choice came to choose love or not, you chose love, and even then, not knowing all you know now, you chose love for the people around you. How much more will I bless you with the gift of love because you ask for it? It is within you, all the love that caused Jesus to die for all, is there with, in your being, because we are there inside you. So, yes to your request to love like us, always yes and more. I told you before, your heart is big enough for the whole body of Christ and it still is growing in love*

*every day, not just for the church, but as you
have witnessed in your dreams, all mankind."*

Thank You!

Thank You, God, for this day. For a merry heart, doing good like a medicine. To be more spirit aware in the moment, to sense Your presence and what is going on (moving as I read the words about You, sometimes I rock back and forth as I do my devotions), I would like to think I am in worship mode as I read about You, like all movement can bring You, worship, praise, adoration.

> *"You live in the Holy of Holies. The mercy seat is open. The coal is in you, the fire pillar. The cloud is in, on, around, over you, always. You are a walking, glowing light of love and glory for Me. Imagine that where you step, flowers grow (in the spirit), but know it can be in the natural also. You have My favor to see, and My word that everywhere you set your foot will be yours. Be that soaking wet sponge and leave residue everywhere you walk. Be the illumination that leaves a glow everywhere you walk."*

Thank You, God, for this day.

> *"When you speak My name (Jesus), it is like*
> *honey flowing from your lips to the hearer.*
> *The Holy Spirit in you is water to the thirsty*
> *souls of those you speak to. My word, the*
> *words that you speak, help to light the path*
> *of those in your care, your family, children,*
> *grandchildren, and all the ones you come in*
> *contact with, who see you as a giver of*
> *My life and light."*

Thank You, God, for this day. Help me to accomplish what I have to do today and not forget one thing, but at the end of the day, be in awe of all I did because of You.

"To help today, praise Me in the morning, praise Me in the noontime, praise Me when the sun goes down. When you keep your thoughts on Me, I can redeem the time for you. Go be fruitful this day and enjoy."

Thank You, God, for this day. Joy, joy—do more things that make you forget to check your phone.

> *"Hold on to Me, for I hold you always. Live this day in My presence as you go and move in this day. Look for Me and see what I have put for you to see."*

4/15/22

Thank You, God, for this day. God, for what you are doing in the community and in all the circles I run in. I believe You are speaking to all, and those with ears to hear are hearing. Thank You for the supernatural spirit realm.

"You will be a voice on the hill, a light that dispels darkness, a wind in the desert, a wheelhouse of treasure, to people everywhere to hear My goodness and love. You glow in it. You flow in it. I support you with My right hand and comfort you."

Thank You, God, for this day. Thank You that I love well all those I meet and in my own family.

4/17/22

Thank You, God, for this day. God, let the love, Your love for my children be so evident today as I feed them and shower them with goodness, and let me be a good representation of You and the love You have for them.

> *"The bird that flies in the sky*
> *The one that flies up so high*
> *If you take wing and begin to sing*
> *In your spirit soar, like that bird before*
> *And see (God) Me open any door."*

4/19/22

Thank You, God, for this day. For life and grace and the ability to run this race You have set before me.

"Let me fill this room, and you, while you just relax and enjoy what I Am doing. I know who needs to be here, and I can take care of all the different needs, and all will feed each other what I have for each one, in one accord. Let the party begin."

4/20/22

Thank You, God, for this day, for your goodness and grace to me. For this growing light and wisdom, I see coming and the joy and gathering spirit in Your people. I also see a hunger that is growing among Your children and the ones who are about to believe.

4/21/22

Thank You, God, for this day.

"Don't let it be hard for you to believe I can say great things to you, about you. I Am always saying these things to all My children. I do love you, and I Am proud of you. I Am thankful for the witness you are for Me. You do look like Jesus, you do touch lives like Jesus, you do love like Jesus. I Am going to bless your socks off. I Am in the day, today, of your business and your land. I Am your source. Be content in Me. Here is My peace because I Am with you. You do live with (God) Me every day."

Thank You, God, for this day. For a lesson in love and seeing others through Your eyes, Your lenses. Thank You for these birds that sit in the trees outside my window. Thank You for my heart and the healing You have put there, making it whole.

4/23/22

Thank You, God, for this day. Help me to complete all I want to get done today and to be mindful of You. Thank You for the joy You have given me as I go about it. To live in every moment "with You" as You are "with me" (Emanuel).

"I can be with you
Open your eyes and see
I never left you
You have always had Me
When the space seems long
And you can't find the throne
You have forgotten, just who you are in Me
I Am always there, open your eyes and see
There is no space in between you and Me
I've always been there, open your
eyes and see!"

Thank You, God, for this day. Let Your light shine and leave residue everywhere I walk, as I live and breathe You in all places.

4/25/22

Thank You, God, for this day, for the opportunity to know You completely, to know what is real and to realize immediately the tricks of the enemy and stop them before they happen. You are God, my God.

> *"And you are daughter, My daughter. There is so much to see and know and you are on the path to enjoy it all. You do hear Me. Don't let anything tell you otherwise. Let Me lead you always. Be encouraged that what your spirit feels will override your flesh. Your heart will delight in Me and the things I have planned for you in this life. See the light, be the light you are, the light as I Am the light."*

Thank You, God, for this day. Thank You that I love well and am so thankful for my mom and family.

Thank You, my soul rests and is kept by You. In You, with You.

Thank You, God, for this day. Thank You for the excitement of seeing the word in a new light and taking it in with renewed hope and love.

4/29/22

Thank You, God, for this day. I am in awe of You and Your way of speaking to my heart and the emotion and glory I feel when I realize You are speaking and doing things in my life. My family's lives. Favor and all wisdom for our business and land.

5/1/22

Thank You, God, for this day. For the insight and wisdom You are bringing to me daily.

5/2/22

Thank You, God, for this day, for loving me so and showing me all that I can do and have in You. As I go forth, let Your light and wisdom shine on others, on my children and their children. I pray their destiny is great and they are bound to heaven, to You, God, with joy and passion, all their days. You are good, and I will praise You always, with every breathe I take, let my praise be heard so loud to Your ears and be a sweet smell to Your nostrils. Thank You for not wasting anything cause there is a lot that needs renewing in my life and heart. I will step on the past and climb higher with You, God, and do all the things You have for me.

*"You do smell good to Me. Your smell is
<u>exquisite</u>. People will be drawn to you because
of it. Remember, 'I smell good on you.'"*

5/3/22

Thank You, God, for this day. God, I pray for the soaking meeting on the thirteenth to be so tangible in that place, touch each heart, and set free all the precious ladies that will be there. My upcoming trip to the beach, let love, joy, and peace be had by all of us.

> *"Don't rush. Let My peace settle on you from the top of your head and run down your entire being, your soul. Let your soul find rest. I will redeem your time. Trust Me. Holy Spirit will bring to remembrance all you need to know and remember for this day, your trip, your packing."*

Thank You, God, for this day. For Your goodness and wisdom. Thank You for my daughter as we celebrate this day of her birth. Thank You for the good ideas in business and a way to be more profitable, to make things less stressful for all of us. The business and the land, I pray for favor, for Your glory, God.

5/9/23

Thank You, God, for this day. God, my soul mate (Larry) has left me here on earth, and I miss that relationship so much. As I seek You in this new journey (path)... I want to know, is it in the plan for me to have a new soul mate? I know that flesh is lonely, and I would so want this, but God, I only want what you want for me. To be what You have planned, so I trust You completely today and always. Help me, LORD, when my trust wavers, to stay strong in You and know You will take care of me always.

Thank You, God, for this day. LORD, don't let me waste this day, this trip, but to seek You completely and see what the next step in my journey, my life, is, to hear so well, to see You, and to follow You always.

5/14/23

Thank You for this day, God. Let me always see You ready to do good in all the situations of our lives. Let me always show You the love that I would love to feel from my children and grandchildren.

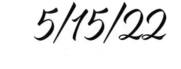

Thank You, God, for this day. God, I need to feel close to You here in this place. Some see You in the waves and sand, and though this is lovely, I am not spending a lot of time there, but here in this house, I am so grateful for and working to make it more beautiful. (I am at the beach in my beach house God has blessed me with.)

Thank You, God, for this day. I want the glory of Your presence to smell so good on me, and I want to seek You with my whole being; to spend time with You is my desire. Peace and rest to me, LORD, this day and always.

5/23/22

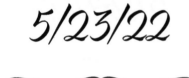

Thank You, God, for this day. I want to seek You and know You even more today, to find in You great mystery and great adventure, LORD!

5/24/22

Thank You, God, for this day. For Your love and goodness to me, even when I feel I can't get the real closeness to You I want in these moments. You are always there, right here with me. Let me see so clearly and BE.

5/25/22

Thank You, God, for this day. The day You speak to me, and I write it down in this book, this journal, that I try with great hopes of writing the accounts of my journey with You in the every day, the now.

> *"Your soul is good, your heart is tender. I Am there within the midst of you."*

5/26/22

Thank You, God, for this day, for Your continued seeking of my soul to engage and commune with You. Speak to me in my sleep, in my wake, in my rest, and in my work. Thank You for the purpose and joy to live, for patience with all people, and for unconditional love. To give You my all and not succumb to flesh and sorrow or self-pity, but to rise up and know who I am and what You have planned for me far exceeds what my mind can see.

Thank You, God, for this day. Let it fall on me, God, or rise up within me. Encounter me, God, this day and every day. Lead me, guide me, glow on me, in me. Fire fall!

Thank You, God, for this day. I want to love well, to walk in this love You have for me, in this walk of life and love and look like Jesus.

6/5/22

Thank You, God, for this day, for the encouragement of friends. Thank You for answering when I ask. I know You speak through me, always, with wisdom and knowledge, that others need to hear, and it is not a planned or rehearsed thing. It is You, Holy Spirit, and I give myself to You all over again to be available. Thank You.

6/6/22

Thank You, God, for this day. Thank You for words from those who hear You, the words "that I Am here, I Am going forward, loss is gone, I Am a eagle, and I will fly."

6/9/22

Thank You, God, for this day. For all I will accomplish, both physical and spiritual.

"I put that notion in you, that every cell in your body, I Am in. I give you the feeling of being invincible in Me because you are. The saying, "Smile like you just got away with something," because you have. It is Me in you. Let it grow bigger and bigger in you. Rest in Me, trust in Me, in every area of your life. Sleep better, rest better, enjoy this work of getting things done. I Am so glad you noticed that I have redeemed time for you because you chose to give Me your morning and know that I Am there all through every moment of your life."

6/10/22

Thank You, God, for this day. God, I give You my life, my children, and their destiny. I give You my business and land to prosper and get glory in.

6/11/22

Thank You, God, for this day. Thank You. I am flying high like an eagle, and we see destiny accomplished in the earth.

Thank You, God, for this day. Let me hear clearly from You today and always. Let my sons feel Your presence and see You, God; let my daughter see and hear You. Let my grandsons be calm and love You, God. Bring the baby girl soon.

6/13/22

Thank You, God, for this day, for rest and peace, and unity in my family. Let me love no matter what, and let them know they are so loved, always. Thank You for favor in this and in my business and land.

6/14/22

Thank You, God, for this day. God, please give me wisdom to help and be there for my family, to look like Jesus in every way and to love others much, and to have peace in all I do.

6/15/22

Thank You, God, for this day. Thank You, God, that You have all the answers, and You give them freely to us who ask. I want to hear You, God, through all the noise of living in this world. With all of the life these little boys are trying to handle, with all of the life my big boys are trying to cope with, and in all of that I pray they turn to You to get help and comfort in those moments.

6/16/22

Thank You, God, for this day. This word came to me this morning as I woke up.

"If I fight in the river, I am tired. If I lay down and float in the river, I am strengthened."

Let me be and do the thing this day that You have for me. I am Yours. I lay all this family at Your feet and ask You to fulfill their destiny in You, in the world. Let me flow in the River today and always. You are there holding my head and keeping me floating.

6/19/22

Thank You, God, for this day. I had a dream about lifting mean people's chins and saying, "Holy Spirit, do what Jesus made a way for." The Spirit came on them and caused them to feel Your glory and caused them to fade away from their evil doings. I believe You, Father, to flow out of me like this to all those around me.

6/20/22

Thank You, God, for this day. Yesterday was Father's Day. Thank You for Your love and grace, for the grace that took us through Father's Day, to know You are the great Father and You never leave.

6/22/22

Thank You, God, for this day. For this day every year for sixty-one years that Larry lived on this earth. I am grateful for the forty-plus ones I had with him, for the woman that I became because of him and most definitely because of You. I am thankful You keep me going in grace and love. Thank You for the future and the plan You have. Thank You for Your patience.

6/25/22

Thank You, God, for this day. For the grace You have given me. I want to leak Jesus everywhere I am, to live in the moments of being fully convinced of Your promises. Wow, what a word, LORD!

> *"Surely My goodness and mercy will follow you and also signs and wonders, for you are My precious daughter, and you do leak with the love I have poured out for you. You are a light and a beacon for all to see. I Am especially fond of you, and yes, you smell good to Me."*

6/26/22

Thank You, God, for this day. For the wonder I feel in my soul, of the mystery of whatever You have for me, I have a sense of wonder and awe; don't ever let that leave me, Father God.

Thank You for this day. For the excitement I feel inside knowing there is an adventure just around the corner to do more with You. Give me wisdom, knowledge to hear and do the thing.

> *"Like a turtle in its shell, I keep coaxing you out, and you come out, and we are going to do this thing, and you retreat some back into the shell. I want to take the shell off completely, so you can see you don't need it or have to have it. You are a vibrant and lively child of Mine, and we will do adventures together. We already are, just stay out of the shell and live, be all I have created you to be, live with the expectation that is within you. Never give up, keep your head up, and trust Me always in all things."*

6/30/22

Thank You, God, for this day. God, I can't get enough of Your amazing love. I have seen Your face, Jesus, and I can't walk away.

Thank You, God, for this day. God, help me to be the best Nana ever. To understand and discipline the right way, and to love well. Touch my sons and daughters with peace and grace and comfort to follow You, LORD, and for my grandchildren to know You, LORD.

Thank You, God, for this day.

The greatest of all Fathers You are, and the God of the universe, the creator, and my friend. I am in awe of all You have done and are doing in me.

Thank You, God, for this day. For the freedom we celebrated today as freedom rings across the land, this nation, the USA. Today, let the truth of Your freedom be so evident.

Thank You, God, for this day. Thank You, God for my children and their children, to know You and trust You and live their lives for You.

Thank You, God, for this day. For the peace of giving You everything I tried to carry. Help me to live this life out without being snarky or self-pity about it. To just simply believe You got me and all that concerns me.

Thank You, God, for this day. For encouragement and grace, Your great grace that is too good to be true but is, it so is.

7/11/22

Thank You, God, for this day, for healing flowing through me. It can't be stopped. It is alive within me. Holy Spirit, do Your thing in my body, my digestion, my stomach and intestines.

"I inhabit your praise. I inhabit you. I Am here,
I see you, hear you. I know you.
Trust me always."

7/12/22

Thank You, God, for this day.

*"Let peace wash over you! Let Me take care
of you! Continue to see yourself in that lake,
floating, and your head in Jesus's hands, also
the picture of you handing everything off your
shoulders into Jesus's hands and Him carrying
it away. I've got you, live, I've got this,
relax in Me."*

7/19/22

Thank You, God, for this day.

"You once had a dream, and there was fog on the mountain. You could not see clearly. As you sat down today and your window was fogged, streamed up, it was hard to see at eye level, but as you looked up, you could see clearly. I want you to see that if you keep your eyes on Me, you will see clearly, don't try to make out what is going on around you at eye level or in the natural.
Look to Me, I Am clear, I Am the way, the truth, the light, and the life, you need and where you should be. Be of good courage and have a light heart and take peace, My peace with you everywhere you go."

7/20/22

Thank You, God, for this day. For the enlightenment You are bringing me to. I desire to have downloaded to me a message for the precious women You bring into my life. I am open to hear You so clearly and to be at rest knowing this is You and not me. I do not want to speak if You are not behind it, in front of it, all around it. I yield myself to You, God, and precious Holy Spirit, to be available and flexible to speak, to touch, to lead, to do whatever You give me to do. I am Yours, I am excited about what You are doing on the earth, and I am here for such a time as this.

Thank You, God, for this day. For the insight You have placed inside of me, giving me wisdom to live and give life to others.

7/27/22

Thank You, God, for this day. For Your glorious love and grace, for my friend as it is the day she was born on this earth. LORD, I give myself, my children, and their children to You again this day to hold us close and never let us go. Bind us all to heaven in Your goodness and love, God. You are love, so much love. I pray all feel this love. I pray for the soaking meeting to be greater and more powerful than I have ever seen. I pray for every lady coming, for the music You pick and put into my hands, for the machine we play it on, for the floor and chairs and building to be so anointed. I pray, God, You open my heart and soul to understand the secret place and ask You to walk with me like You walked with Adam in the garden.

"Come on, precious, you know I will. All these things I have put before you to pick up and take hold of, you can, you will, and I Am with you. I have you and yours, and I will shine and show you the way all the days, and we will see My glory together in all these things. You are favored and blessed by Me, keep on keeping on, and listen for My urging to move this way and

that, hear My voice cause you do, and I will tell you the things of mystery you so want to hear, and be there always as I Am. I hear you, I see you, I hold you, let all the things go and rest in Me this day and all the days to come. Be My mouthpiece for the precious ones you have the honor and pleasure to touch in your circles and outside of them too."

7/28/22

Thank You, God, for this day. Thank You for the download of Your precious word this morning to pour over the ladies on Friday night. Let it be so anointed and tangible in the soaking.

> *"You are the garden. You are the vineyard. I Am the vinedresser. I love My garden, My vines, My precious ones. I will take care of you. You will bloom and bring forth fruit and feed the hungry in My name. Thank you for trusting Me with all in every area of your life. I Am here, right here with you. I see you, I hear you, I honor My word!"*

7/29/22

Thank You, God, for this day, for Your wisdom and clear thinking to help with all the needs of the ones around me. With You leading and giving the solutions, this is not a hard thing. I give myself to You to speak to, to lead, and guide to help in any way You would have me to.

7/30/22

Thank You, God, for this day. The hope and joy and expectation growing in my chest, my soul, my most inner parts to walk with You and be in the same room, the same world as You are, the same breath, in this body. To be in the secret place and walk with You like You walked with Adam in the garden.

Thank You, God, for this day. And all the days of my life. I rest and trust in You, God. I give myself to You. Lead me and guide me into all truth. Let me speak with grace and truth and rhema flowing out of my mouth and touch others for Your glory.

8/2/22

Thank You, God, for this day. Speak, LORD! I will write it.

"For the glory is given without rebuke,
For the manner of life, you can't refute,
Be all there is to be today,
Don't let anything stand in your way
Live out your best life in My presence
Let the world around you see evidence
I have called you higher still,
There is no cost, no paying the till
My love for you is strong and true
You hear Me, child, and I see you."

8/9/22

Thank You, God, for this day.

*"This day is a day dedicated to Me as all days
should be. Walk with Me today. Let Me lead
you and whisper in your ear, this day, and be
purposeful to listen and to be expectant in Me.
For you will know today the things you long
for to be all I have called you to. Let no fear or
doubt come in and take any of your peace and
desire I have placed there within you. You hear
Me, and I see you! Girl, I got you!"*

I have a choice to ride the glory wave of Yours, God, or a
grief wave of pain and hurt. I choose You, God. May have
to choose every day, several times a day, but I choose You
and peace and comfort from Your heart.

8/10/22

Thank You, God, for this day, for the days before and after this day. I am grateful for everyone, for the breath in my lungs, and for the great plan You have for me on this earth.

Thank You, God, for this day. For the light and life that pours out of me and all around me to give me power and strength in all things.

8/15/22

Thank You, God, for this day. For Your love that abounds in me and from me, let it always be so.

To love and give love and be who You have called me to.

Thank You, God, for this day. For the insight to see, hear, and follow after You. To know Your voice, to see Your face, and to hear. Your directions clearly, like tell me what it means that " I don't have to finish what he started, and what is next for me?"

Thank You, God, for this day, for the grace and love to walk out the every day and the special day things, to look and be like Jesus.

Thank You, God, for this day. For Your love and goodness to me, for Your freedom and wisdom.

Thank You, God, for this day. For You're being absolutely brilliant.

8/29/22

Thank You, God, for this day. It represents the day we married. Thank You for those forty years, God. I remember the good, the blessings, and embrace You, God, to heal my heart and be who You have put me here to be.

Thank You, God, for this day. Thank You for my children who blessed me and came to celebrate me last night on a day that could have brought tears, but laughter came to us all.

8/31/22

Thank You, God, for this day, for Your love and kindness to me, for loving me so well and leading my life by You. God, there are moments that I trust and "feel" it's going to be okay. You have me. You've got this. I am patient to wait and know You have the best for me. And then, some moments, I "feel" like I can't wait till I have someone to love me, here in the flesh on earth. I am sorry, God, that my body goes to these "feelings" and thoughts of a woman. I cry out for Your help and peace in these times of weakness and trust You again to take care of me in every moment and that all things, the good, the bad, the ugly, work for my good because You don't waste anything. I am growing and standing in the truth that You can take of it all. I am Yours, and You are mine.

> *"Rest in Me today, triggers come and triggers go. But I remain always holding you in the palm of My hand. I did remind you today that I Am yours, and you are Mine! Believe it, walk in it, sit in it, sleep in it. It's okay to let the love, passion and compassion you feel ooze out of you in all situations and with all people. I Am in that, you know it, you 'feel' it. It's okay to 'feel.' I created it, so enjoy it. The best is yet to come. Rest in that."*

9/3/22

Thank You, God, for this day. For people who love me and send help my way. For favor with these that bring help. Thank You for this favor and for Yours that I live with every single day of my life. I am in awe of your care for me and pray that I see this revealed in my life always and give You, God, all the glory and honor and praise for all of this.

9/5/22

Thank You, God, for this day. Thank You for the seed You have planted in me. Keep adding to it, and I will soon understand the exacts of what You have called me to. I will follow Your directions and be all You are leading me on for.

The march is underway, and I am here today to be and go, to do and receive all I hear You say, lead on my good and great friend, my love and comforter. I hear, I write and will be the voice you have put inside of me.

9/6/22

Thank You, God, for this day. God, for the future, You have for me. Thank You that You love me and are there for me in my weak moments of flesh that I battle to stay above the waves and trust You completely. I praise You and bless Your name in all the times I need You so. Touch my children, hold them close, and be real to them. Give them a love that surpasses what their parents had, and that will be so great a love, but help them to put You first always, in the middle of these relationships.

9/8/22

Thank You, God, for this day. For the wisdom and rhema You are giving me. Help me, God, to stop saying, "I am broken," because You gave me a tender heart. My heart is Yours, and with the feelings of flesh of a woman and all that contains, to be loved and touched and treated like a queen on the earth. I am Your queen, God, and You love me completely. You know what I need, and You take care of me, so once again, I rest in the trust I have in You. You are greater than any feeling or hormone in my body, greater than any need. You are mine, and I am Yours, and You keep reminding me of that. Thank You.

9/10/22

Thank You, God, for this day. Thank You for all the days of my life and the peace and trust I have because of You, God. Lead me to be the best me on the earth I can be. Let me love well, and to love myself well, to take care of this body and soul with the knowledge that You take care of it above all.

As I walk through this journey of life, You are with me. With my head up or down, You are there. Leading me always and knowing You care. Always reminding me, here in this life, I am free! Free to live the way You have planned and help me to be.

Thank You, God, for this day. The day You have made. I am in tears today and can't really pinpoint the reason. Is it near the anniversary mark of two years? Is it the tears of love and wanting those unlovely to be loved? Is it the business and the close race of selling and buying to make a profit and not come up short? Is it the whole dynamics of family business and not knowing what each other thinks or feels? God, please take care of it all, business, land, rentals, my family, me!

9/16/22

Thank You, God, for this day. I took my rings off today. Thank you for all the grace and peace you have put in my soul, to live in this world knowing I Am in that world also and wanting to believe that so completely. Knowing I can trust You with everything in me. My heart, my soul, my mind, longs for You God, to be so real, so tangible in my life.

Thank You, God, for this day and every day. You are my days, my nights, my breath. Let me see this so clearly and react in the way You have for me to.

When I sit right here in the midst of Your presence, looking into the hope of Your vastness, I hear the whisper of Your voice nudging me on to enter in the song, the comfort, the peace of Your bliss. I am getting acquainted with and longing for Your tone! And with complete trust in You, I can never go wrong!

9/18/22

Thank You, God, for this day. For Your love and grace that covers me, always and opens my eyes to see the things You have put in front of me, favor and blessings.

9/19/22

Thank You, God, for this day. For Your wisdom and truth, let it be so big in me. To hear, to see, to understand, to love so well, and to look like Jesus.

9/20/22

Thank You, God, for this day. For wisdom and belief in You and the glory that surrounds me flows out of me onto others, or objects to touch others, just like the aprons from the apostle Paul.

Thank You, God, for this day. For the favor and grace You so gladly give us. I am in awe of You and believe and trust You completely, or I want to, and pray I do.

When the larks of leaven sing a song so sweet that the chorus silence and listen to the praise of Your glory, the adoration, and awe, no ear can contain it, no voice imitate it, only those who know what the one who deserves all praise has done for them!

Thank You, God, for this day, for the power and grace to walk it like You have planned me to. I am Yours, and You are mine.

"The times you thank Me, in these moments of solitude... You are not alone. You were never alone. What you think is solitude is a place you can hear Me clearly. In the stillness, I Am there, always there. Thank you for listening."

9/23/22

Thank You, God, for this day. For the trip with my friends to run away, so to speak, even though I know I can't, but to just be busy on the twenty-fourth and not let heartache overtake me in any way. I pray for my children to have peace and comfort in their hearts.

> *"All these things are yours. I have provided*
> *them for you, to you and yours. All you have*
> *to do is ask, but even before you do, I have*
> *already sent them. Just trust and believe Me.*
> *You are Mine, and I Am yours, now and always.*
> *There is no end. What I started, I will complete*
> *in you. You are a good, good daughter, and*
> *I love you brilliantly. My love for you knows*
> *no bounds, no obstacles. There is nothing in*
> *between us, nothing. I Am right*
> *here right now!"*

Thank You, God, for this day. This is the anniversary of two years of living without Larry here but there with You, God. Thank You for healing my heart more and more each and every day. Closer and closer to You, learning to walk in You and be fulfilled in Your presence.

9/26/22

Thank You, God, for this day.

There is a stream in a meadow, and there I find a peace and calm that only You can bring as I sit and reflect on the things You have done in my life. I try to see the things coming to me. I am in awe of You, my King and Creator, Father of my soul and life.

9/30/22

Thank You, God, for this day.

For the way You love me and all You do. Letting me see You in and on everything. Turning things around for my good. Bringing favor in my life, with friends, family, and workers to help with all my needs, always.

Thank You, God, for this day, for the rest of my life on earth and for eternity.

Every moment, God, You are watching me, loving me, and making all things new. You are the great and awesome God, creator of my universe and all that consists of. There is none like You before or after this life on earth, and I will always live because I am Yours, and You are mine.

You make this world go round, and I am in awe of You and the great love You have for me. Thank You for the passion You have put inside me.

10/3/22

Thank You, God, for this day. God, help me to be and feel successful today in all I do. I need to accomplish stuff in my house, in my life, and also hear Your voice.

> *"'Hear Me.' Hear Me? You hear Me, you sense, you move in Me. You are learning and growing and being in the secret place, dwelling, living, being here with Me."*
> *'Hear You.' I hear you, I see you, I know what you need. I know you love big and need to put that love on someone. We will overcome together. I have promised. I have given you what you need. You will see."*

10/4/22

Thank You, God, for this day.

"There is a place in time 'only because you focus on time,' I do not, but in time, you will see all I see right now. Don't give up; don't be discouraged because I have got you. Always have and always will. Keep pressing in on the glory, carrying, touching, releasing power truth, cause I will move in that. I will be in the residue of your touch, shadow, clothing, cause what you touch, I touch, what you love, I love, because I first loved you, you are able to love. Enjoy this day."

Thank You, God, for this day. Thank You for the insight to see and hear what You are saying to me. Truth, anointing, glory carrier, touch, heal, deliver.

Thank You, God, for this day. For Your truth and wisdom that I so long to walk in, live in always. Help me not to say, "I don't have discernment," because… God, I have You, I have Holy Spirit in me, and He has every gift there is, so I have all gifts available to me when the need arises.

10/11/22

Thank You, God, for this day, for rhema words to flow from You, God, to me, for wisdom and knowledge to be on time all the time. For rest and calm for my children in the midst of chaos. To trust in You and know You have our backs.

Thank You, God, for this day. Thank You for not leaving me for a minute. Thank You that You know and have a future and hope for me, even if I feel or think in all different fashions. I want to think like You, to trust in You, to be okay, and not feel needy. I need You only and letting You direct the rest of my life.

10/13/22

Thank You, God, for this day. The day You have made, the day I rejoice in You to the praise of Your glory.

What is the thought that goes through my mind when I quiet myself before You? A lark, what is a lark, besides a bird that flies in my head when I want to listen, in Your presence?

Are You calling me Your songbird?

Or inviting me on a quest or adventure?

Or want me to have fun?

LORD, I want all three of these to be true. For all are requests or commands in Your word.

"Sing unto the LORD a new song" (Psalm 96:1).
"Come follow Me" (Matthew 4:12–25).
"Eat, drink and enjoy life, it is a gift from God"
(Ecclesiastes 8:15, 3:12).

Thank You, God, for this day. For the ideas, You put into me, if this is what You want me to do on October 30, then make it happen because I cannot do it on my own, and I know I am never on my own because You will never leave me. Open my ears, eyes, and heart to pour that love on other women who need to be closer to You than ever before.

10/17/22

Thank You, God, for this day. Thank You for the wisdom and knowledge that You give me daily and the grease to see Your face and be what You have called me to. I surrender my will, my agenda, to You in everything, ever knowing I need to do this every day and sometimes more than once. I long to be in Your presence, to taste Your glory, Your weighed touch. I am over the numbness of grief or whatever the heaviness of not feeling is. I release it to You so that in every moment, I can enter in and be with You. To discover all the gifts in all the moments that they are needed.

"The branches in your life entwine around the people you love, and the fruit of goodness and grace I have given you grow big and ripe for those to choose and enjoy and even be able to grow from. You are a light I have put on a hill for all to see. You are the lamp. I Am the light. We will see the dreams and hopes be fulfilled in the manner I have planned to. I plant you, and you grow, and a harvest is had by those around you because you hear Me. Always be sensitive to My voice. I Am yours, and you are Mine!"

10/19/22

Thank You, God, for this day. For the beauty that is displayed all over the trees, the sky, my children, and grandchildren. I am in awe of You. I want to live in moments of trusting You so completely to make our lives what You have planned.

> *"In you, I live and breathe and move. You don't always feel it, but, hey, you know I don't go by feelings. I Am a force. I Am a moving being of light and love. Go beyond feeling, beyond logic, and find Me right there with you. Speak, believe and see, just what you said. I Am for you, not against you. I Am greater in you than who is in the world. I have your best interest in My heart, to see you succeed and have a future of good."*

Thank You, God, for this day. And for seeing a different perspective, "Yours" in all things, to love like Jesus in all things.

Thank You, God, for this day. For the honor to pray and ask for help for me and others, to believe that You are for me and not against me, and You are so much greater.

I have looked beyond the veil. I have seen and felt the joy of complete trust. I want to live in this arena every moment of my life, to move out of it, to speak, and to teach from it.

10/27/22

Thank You, God, for this day. Thank You for these words for my friend this day. God, everyone wants to be loved and respected in their relationships.

"When we stand in the path of indecision

Is there a right or wrong way?

God is with us in all things, and He will take whatever and make us whole again.

When our puzzle pieces are shattered and strewn,

He reshapes them and makes us new.

Take heart and be of good cheer, whether here or there. God is with you."

Thank You, God, for this day. Thank You for Sunday school. I am so in awe of the anointing and grace You pour on me and out of me to look like Jesus and to have people feel Your touch in the midst. I feel You and know You are leading me and directing my words with grace. Holy Spirit, thank You for bringing rhema as You speak to me and through me.

11/1/22

Thank You, God, for this day and all the days of my life, my children's life, and their children and their children. I will declare my lineage to You, God, binding them to heaven.

I've heard it said that a man would climb a mountain just to be with the one he loves! This song sung by Third Day I listen to and cry every time since my man went to heaven. The song speaks of Jesus's great love for us and the lengths He would and did go for us just to be with us. I have wondered since losing my husband from this world, how men and women could not love the way God has so clearly planned in the word. Maybe because of grief, I see things as being petty, in the disagreements of marriage. What would you do to keep someone you might lose? Ephesians 5:25 says, "Husbands love your wives like Christ loved the church." What did He do for the church? He died for it. What will you do to keep those you love? Let passion and compassion guide you and live in the fullness of God.

11/2/22

Thank You, God, for this day.

"Jesus stooped, and He wrote in the sand
She was delivered by the work of His hand
Jesus stooped when carried the cross
He made a way to deliver the lost
Will you stoop to free your fellow man
With His love and grace, yes, you can
Be the light; the world needs to see
Shine in the darkness, go set people free
Jesus in you is the hope for the world
Every man, every woman, boy and girl
When we all are one, and the night is gone
We will worship the King on His throne."

11/3/22

Thank You, God, for this and day.

"In a moment things can change
In a moment when you speak my name
Don't let fear and doubt reclaim
Blow them away and never be the same
My heart for you is always a flame
To never leave and to remain
Standing on the edge of forever
Standing on the edge of time
Standing on the edge of forever
My heart is Yours, and Yours is mine."

11/5/22

Thank You, God, for this day, for Your presence in my life. Lead me, guide me in all my steps to follow You. Touch my kids today to feel Your touch on their lives, work in all things for our good. We trust You, God.

"Falling into Your arms,
I am falling on the cornerstone,
for You are strong and I belong,
Falling into Your arms,
where trust is conceivable, and hope is
believable,
Falling into Your arms."

Thank You, God, for this day. Thank You for the honor to stand in for my children till they see You in all Your glory, loving them. I am blessed to pray for them in their jobs, their parenting, their marriages, their finances, their peace of mind, their health, their fertility, their happiness and joy. To pray favor on their lives to see them prosper in all they do. I bind them to heaven and thank You for each one of them, My children, that You so awesomely gave to me with the wisdom to pray for them. Thank You for favor and blessings on my business and rentals. Take care of me and my family. I trust You, God, I believe You. God, I know You work all things for my good, all things!

Thank You, God, for this day. Give us the eyes to see the peace You have poured out on us. Thank You for favor on all our business endeavors, for Your glory, let us not lose sight of this. That it is all for You, all Yours, we are Yours, and You are ours. Such love as we have never known is revealed to us on the daily. To love, to live, to laugh, to see, to feel, to touch all in Your name Jesus!

11/8/22

Thank You, God, for this day. Thank You for Your faithfulness to me.

"I'm right here in Your presence O my God,
I'm right here in Your presence O my God,
I'm right here in Your presence, right here in
Your presence,
Speak to me in Your presence, O my God.
Lift your ear in My presence and you will hear,
Lift your ear in My presence and you will hear,
Be still and know that I Am your God,
Be still and know, Be still and know,
Be still and know that I Am your God.
I Am here and you are not alone,
I Am here, I Am here, I Am here.
I Am here and you are not alone."
Song *God Gave Me*

Thank You, God, for this day. Thank You for the trust You have given me, to trust You completely. I fall into Your arms and rest because You are my everything. In You, I live and breathe and have my being.

11/10/22

Thank You, God, for this day. Thank You for favor in all situations.

You are the God from whom all blessings flow. You are the God who sees me here below. You are the God who says, " I love you." You give me words to say, "I love You too."

11/11/22

Thank You, God, for this day. Thank You for goodness and grace, for simply believing what You have revealed to me. I am seated in heavenly places with You. Thank You for rescuing me. Rescue me every day. Thank You, You hear me.

Thank You, God, for this day.

Whisper. Have you heard the whisper? In the night, wake from sleep? In the meadow, appreciating peace? Have you heard the whisper? In the eyes of a baby, in the touch of a friend. Have you heard the whisper of the Creator of the universe? It is all around you, in the wind, in the trees, in the water running free. It is in you. It is in me. We are the whisper He has put in the earth, for all to hear, telling the sweet story of why God came near.

11/14/22

Thank You, God, for this day. The day You have made. Thank You for the adamant state of my heart and soul to trust You and not waver, to rest in Your love and care, as You promised to take care of me. I trust You with the business, my children, and their children. I trust You with all my family, my mom, my sister and her family. Let me stay in the secret place where the enemy can't even find me. To rest in the shadow of Your wings, the embrace of Your strong arms, the love that You so freely and greatly pour out on me.

"Do you ever wonder where it is, this place called secret? It is simple, so very simple, to sit in My presence and commune with Me, I see you, I hear you, I know your every move. It is not difficult to hear Me, see Me, and know My moves too."

Thank You, God, for this day. Thank You that I am Your daughter, a woman seeking after You.

"You are a banner on a hill, walking, shining in My will. I propose to you this day, live your best life as you walk in the way. I Am standing, cheering you on. You are also seated next to Me on the throne. Your enemy is under your feet. It's a good day to harvest the wheat to gather the sheep."

11/16/22

Thank You, God, for this day. Thank You for the goodness in my life.

"Come walk in the woods with Me.
Sit and talk in the woods with Me.
There is peace in the woods with Me.
There is calm in the woods with Me.
No matter where you are at, there is all this, as
long as you are with Me."

11/17/22

Thank You, God, for this day. Thank You for the grace and help You have given me all the days of my life. Pie in the sky! I Believe!

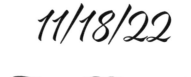

Thank You, God, for this day. God, as we sit down to talk about the path we need to go on, please, Holy Spirit, be in the midst of our conversation, touch our hearts to hear and our minds to understand what needs to be done in the business. Go ahead and make a way for us. Let us receive the peace and rest You have poured on us.

God, I trust You. I say it again today. My whole life is found in Your love. Today is a day I give up my hands. I surrender to You, God, is what I should do always. So let it be a giving up to You to let You have it all, and not giving up of my sanity but taking back my confidence in You.

11/19/22

Thank You, God, for this day.

*"There is no need to say anything. I know, I
see. I have you in My hands. Rest in Me, trust
Me to do what you cannot. To take what seems
impossible and make it work in your favor. Let
your mind rest on Me. Let Me orchestrate the
future. Stop going down every path you can
think of. Just breathe, just stay
in the secret place."*

Thank You, God, for this day.

Release in me the power to be. To walk this path and to bow the knee. Only to You and to You alone. Because You are the King, the One on the throne.

11/21/22

Thank You, God, for this day. Thank You for the shift, the answers that You bring in the night or day and speak to me, to my children about the business, and You work in all areas of our lives.

11/22/22

Thank You, God, for this day. The day You made for us to rejoice in and be glad.

*"Rest in what is yours today, life and liberty.
Seize the day, the hope, your dreams. The way
you hold to the promises is a tribute to the trust
you have for Me. Keep the belief you have in
Me, and you will see those come to you
because you are Mine."*

11/23/22

Thank You, God, for this day.

Today's word was stand in the midst/mist. Not knowing which midst/mist for sure. I have defined both.

Midst: middle point, surrounded.

Mist: cloud, cover with.

I want both. To be covered by God's cloud and also to be in the middle of His glory, His will, His love, His grace, His presence.

A song I wrote:

"Standing in the midst/mist 3x... forever

Living in the bliss of standing in the midst/mist 2x... forever"

11/25/22

Thank You, God, for this day.

"Burning in the oil of Your salvation," a word I heard.

A song we used to sing years ago: "Give me oil in my lamp, keep me burning..."

11/26/22

Thank You, God, for this day.

As the smoke rises in the morning sun and the shadows of the forest fall across the yard, the beauty of nature brings comfort to my soul and peace to my past. Thank You, God, for Your presence in all these things, drawing me ever closer to You and the joy You bring.

> *"I see you, I have always seen you,*
> *and I will always see you."*

Thank You, God, for this day. Thank You for Your goodness and forgiveness.

Thank You, God, for this day. Thank You for the restoration of all things.

There is a star that shines in Bethlehem, bold and bright and free, a reminder of the King of kings, that came and died for me, and rose and shines brighter than this star, and He shines inside of me.

11/29/22

Thank You, God, for this day. Thank You for the deep wisdom and knowledge to know You.

Word of the day—*yada*, in Hebrew means to "know", not only the knowledge of God, it is also knowing God, knowing You.

> *"Where the weary lay their head, in the middle of the rest, I have placed there to relieve the stress, the angst, the woe, I will release all the bad, the trauma, the pain, and bless their heads, with peace that passes all understanding and you will be the sons of God, I have called you to."*

11/30/22

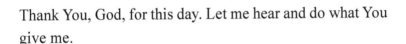

Thank You, God, for this day. Let me hear and do what You give me.

"As the dew drops in the vastness of a lake,
there are ripples. Make no mistake, you are
more than a drop of dew. Your ripples in this
world reach far and wide. I Am pleased to be
by your side, always and forever. Each moment
with you is a new adventure
I will see you through."

Word of the day—"breeze": easy to do, come and go in a lighthearted manner, gentle wind.

12/1/22

Thank You, God, for this day. Thank You for speaking to me and through me. I am Yours, and You are mine.

"There are three, three in one, three forces flowing into you. Not just one, but three: the Father, the Son, the Holy Spirit."

Thank You, God, for this day, matriarch: A woman who is the head of a family or tribe. I believe this, LORD. Help me to do even more! (This word was spoken at a prayer group that I am a part of.)

12/3/22

Thank You, God, for this day.

As the rain falls and soaks the ground, so Your presence falls on me to soak my soul. The ground doesn't close itself off from the saturation of the refreshing, and neither will I. I purposely open every pore and space for You, my God, to flow into and cover me, nourish me.

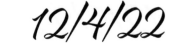

Thank You, God, for this day. God, I am seeking the secret place where I am hidden in You. The place I walk out this earth walk in Your perfect will and pleasure. To touch, to speak, to be in You completely. To be fully known by You and to know You fully. To hear, to receive, to understand.

12/5/22

Thank You, God, for this day. Thank You for speaking to me, for words that only You could give me, and for revealing the meaning of all things. Thank You for trust and the compassion You give me, for being careful with me and loving me in my mess ups.

12/6/22

Thank You, God, for this day. Thank You for blessing me with a dream of my daddy on the day he was born on the earth. Thank You for the reminders of You praying for me always. If we have Jesus praying for us, how can we fail? We can't! For greater is He that is in us than He that is in the world.

Thank You, God, for this day.

God, You plant in us to see a harvest, and if an earthly man can reap a harvest from dirt and seeds, how much more God the creator can plant in us, and it will come to pass. We will grow fruit because He said it, He promised it. We will reap in due season if we don't grow weary and faint.

Thank You, God, for this day. LORD, I want intimacy with You, to be fully known, to share that love and knowing with those around me.

12/11/22

Thank You, God, for this day. Thank You for being in the midst as we talk today about what to do about the business. We, my daughter, son, and I, have kept the business going for two years after my husband passed. It is getting to be too much to keep up with the crew, so today, we have to let workers go, which is very hard to do, but there is no other choice. God has helped us in this, and we are grateful for the weight that has been lifted. Believing Him to prosper all we set our hands to.

12/12/22

Thank You, God, for this day. Thank You for all the truth You fill me with. Peace, love, and grace are mine. I am taken care of by You. Restore my soul and my heart.

"You dwell in the secret place of My most high, in Me. Don't let life or circumstance dictate to you. It is a trick to keep you down; don't let it. See what I see, hear what I hear. I Am telling you, hold on, deliverance is coming, it is here. You are an overcomer in the middle of all. You hear Me and obey. I honor that. Continue on, we've got this."

12/14/22

Thank You, God, for this day. Let joy and light leak out all over the people, precious people today. To bring peace and love and brighten their day,

In the stillness of the day, when no birds are out at play, is this what it means "to be still and know"? Are You here? Do You hear? Do I stay, do I go? I know, I know. You never leave. With all I am, I want to believe!

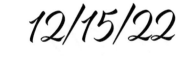

Thank You, God, for this day.

I have noticed that in the midst of circumstance and confusion, if your heart is toward God, you can hear Him and obey. These are the steps in defeating the devil and turning around the mess that is trying to shut you down. This is a very encouraging discovery in my point of view that I can separate spirit and flesh and soon bring my whole in agreement and see with God's perspective.

12/16/22

Thank You, God, for this day. Thank You for Your love and grace. You pour out on me the wisdom I need for this day and the touch and speech to everyone around me.

Word of the day—"diecast": to pour hot metal or plastic into and cast to make an image. You are the potter, I am the clay. You mold me and make me look like Jesus. (Isaiah 64:8)

12/19/22

Thank You, God, for this day. Open my eyes, my ears, my heart. I always want to hear You.

"The blade of grass grows up from the earth. Have you noticed how everything reaches up as it grows, getting taller toward the sky, the heavens? They are reaching for Me, the trees, the flowers, all trying to get My attention. Out of all these beautiful things, the ones who have My most intense attention are you and those who are reaching, seeking, trying to see My face, yearning to be in the secret place."

12/20/22

Thank You, God, for this day. Let me always be grateful to You, God, for every breath and movement in my being, for my family, that Larry is safe within Your arms, that You have my back always. I am thankful for all these things.

> "When the leaves have fallen, and the trees are bare, look at it as preparing, and don't give it a care. I know what I Am doing. I have done it for so long. Let it be a picture of peace and quiet. Put your trust in Me, and you can't go wrong! I Am the maker, creator, master of it all. I was here before. I was hereafter. I made a way beyond the fall. Jesus is the answer, Jesus is the man, let your heart rest in Me, trust Me, I have a plan!"

Thank You, God, for this day. Thank You for the love You give me.

First love, and how do I attain it? To fall head over heels in love with Jesus has been my answer in the past, and maybe it is the answer. I want to be sure. I want to walk in the laid-down self, pick up and put on Jesus life to the fullness, to know and accept that I am a walking, talking vessel that Christ is in, that Holy Spirit is in, that I hear from You, Father God, and because of that, love abounds big in me.

Word of the day—"reciprocate": to give, to feel in return.

12/23/22

Thank You, God, for this day. Thank You for what You have for me and my household, my family. Keep us safe always, LORD. Keep the power on and the trees in the ground on this windy, cold day.

The wind roars out my window. The sun shines on my face through the glass pane as I sit here in Your presence, giving You this day and all it entails. I am safe in Your arms.

Thank You, God, for this day. Thank You for loving me and guiding me along the way. As a sheep in the pasture, You lead me, protect me, give me food and water to sustain me. You comfort me and care for me. Let my soul and flesh finally receive this as it is the truth and reality of this life and the world to come.

Thank You, God, for this day. The day we celebrate Jesus's birth, His coming here to rescue us. So very thankful for You.

"I sit in this moment looking back over the years and Christmas's past. The plays, the special services, the dress. In all of this, I see You were always right here inside of me, not the hustle and bustle, the grand designs, but here in my heart waiting all the time."

12/26/22

Thank You, God, for this day.

"Sometimes you don't hear the words, but your heart melts a little because you read that He hears your cries and He comes down to do something about your situation. That is love. That is the definition of a good daddy, one who picks you up when you fall and holds you in the middle of the mess. Being there when no one else is. Rise up above the mess and see what He sees. Let His perception be yours. It will change your life."

Wrote these lyrics to the tune of a song, "Bicycle Built for Two."

"Jesus, Jesus, give me an answer, do, I'm half crazy when I don't listen to you.

Help me, Jesus, when I act like I don't have a clue.

Cause it's so sweet upon the seat in the heavenly place with you."

Thank You, God, for this day, and all the days before and beyond today.

"My eye is on the sparrow, but My eye is on you more, my eye is on the dragonfly, but I will watch you soar, My eye is on the lily, but your fragrance pleases Me. My eye is on the sunrise, but My light in you is key. It's the light, the sounds, that you make, that delight the heart in Me. Though My eye is on many things, it's on you that joy brings, so rest in the knowledge that you are Mine, and that's what makes you sing."

12/28/22

Thank You, God, for this day.

When I lay my life down for another when I look like Jesus in this way, it will help a sister or brother. It is doing what the Father would say.

Wisdom in the night. You tell me what to do. (Psalm 16:7)

I am thankful!

12/30/22

Thank You, God, for this day. This year is coming to an end. Thank You for the expectation in the coming new year. Let me walk in the destiny You have for me and encounter the tangible touch from You daily.

12/31/22

Thank You, God, for this day. Give me wisdom and the ability to accomplish today all in the natural and the spiritual, for I live in two worlds, and I want to respond as such.

"The trees are barren, the leaves are dead,
winter is here, and the sight is drear, but the
spring is coming and what life it brings, rest in
this season, gather up the word, for when the
time comes, you will be heard."

#

On 6/28/23, I wrote as I had just finished the copying of the manuscript for this book, Thank You, God, for this day. The book is finished.

> *"The book is not done. Your life is the book. You have only just begun. Live your life to the fullest in all my ways. There will be pages to write. There will be paragraphs for days. I Am in you, and you are in Me. There will be no end to what you will see. So hear it and dream it, and write it all down. There are an abundance of stories in Me to be found."*

When I finished my book and was ready to send it to the publisher, this came to me. This is true for me, for you. So pick up those pens and write the story God is giving you.

Special thanks to Krista Bryant Sisk for the technical support and for putting this book into PDF form to send to the publisher. And for all you do, I am grateful!

Also, thank you to Zoiey Markle for the hours spent with me working on the edited manuscript.

Milton Keynes UK
Ingram Content Group UK Ltd.
UKHW011818090224
437558UK00013B/551